THE ENEMY WE KILLED, MY FRIEND

Photo taken through U-156 periscope, thirty seconds after the torpedo was fired, detonating against the hull of *Quebec City*.

THE ENEMY WE KILLED,
MY FRIEND

David C. Jones

First Impression—1999

ISBN 1 85902 624 9

The maps on p. 12 and p. 127 are the work of Alan Bradley.

Printed in Wales at
Gomer Press, Llandysul, Ceredigion

I am the enemy you killed, my friend.
I knew you in the dark: for so you frowned
Yesterday through me as you jabbed and killed.
I parried; but my hands were loath and cold.
Let us sleep now . . .

from 'Strange Meeting', Wilfred Owen

In a dream, Owen finds himself in hell, where he meets a German soldier who talks with him about 'the truth untold, the pity of war, the pity war distilled.' He wishes that all the bloodshed could be washed clean with water 'from sweet wells . . . with truths that lie too deep for taint.'

To my family, past and present, especially my dear Mother, fondly remembered and known as 'Mam Jones', who was highly respected for her determination and guidance. Also my dear wife Edwina and daughter Anne for their most valued encouragement and support, over a period of three and a half years of writing and archive research.

Finally to my lifelong friend and fellow survivor, Captain Michael George Terryl Hughes, Master Mariner, sadly now deceased, who was so interested in all my research and so delighted that our story was to be told.

This book is a personal tribute to all who served in the Battle of the Atlantic Ocean. They asked little quarter and gave none. Skill, endurance and courage were common to friend and foe, all contending with nature's elements of storms and mountainous seas. A war at sea demanded everything of all participants, often beyond the call of duty.

'WITH THE GOING DOWN OF THE SUN AND IN THE MORNING, WE WILL REMEMBER THEM'

Prologue

Saturday 19 September 1942. 15.46. The British flag S.S. *Quebec City*, a cargo vessel of 10,000 tons, was on passage home to the U.K., fully laden with Egyptian cotton seed and baled cotton, goods essential to the survival of Fortress Britain.

She had loaded at the port of Alexandria, by a system that seemed little changed since the Pharaohs built their pyramids. In choking heat and humidity, hundreds, thousands perhaps, of Arab labourers in white smocks that covered them from shoulders to ankles carried on their backs the cotton seed in its hessian sacks. Up the steep planks from quayside to main deck they ran, a line of busy ants, tipping their burdens into the open hatches on the fore and after decks, running back for more. Back-breaking labour, shift work, twenty-four hours a day.

The only 'safe' route back to the U.K. was east to Port Said, through the Suez Canal and Red Sea to the Indian Ocean, then south down the length of Africa to the Cape of Good Hope before turning northwards home through the Atlantic – a very long haul indeed compared to the peace-time route west through the Mediterranean to Gibraltar. But 1942 was the year of the Malta Convoys: the combined Axis forces of Germany and Italy dominated the eastern Mediterranean from their bases in Tunisia, Libya and occupied Greece, Crete and Cyprus – and Rommel was threatening Egypt itself.

From Cape Town, the route was to Freetown, Sierra Leone, where the West African Royal Naval Base provided an assembly point for convoys to be escorted home. The *Quebec City* had zig-zagged her way down the Red Sea and Indian Ocean and, uneventfully in spite of enemy activity in these areas, into the South Atlantic. Weather conditions were typical for just south of the Equator: light northeast breeze with a slight sea, cloudless blue sky, humid and with an ambient temperature at midday of 88°F. The vessel's position, at 15.46 hours, was Latitude 2° 12′ South, Longitude 17° 36′ West, some 450 miles northwest of the Ascension Islands and 1,200 miles south-west of the nearest mainland, the west coast of Africa and the coastline of Liberia.

I had had a hard and sticky morning of routine Saturday duties and would have welcomed a long, cool shower. I was obliged to forgo my scheduled lunch-break at 12.30 owing to extra work commitments before the vessel's arrival at Freetown. Like the rest of the crew, I had realised, from the increased activity on the bridge, that the captain and senior officers were aware of some enemy action in the neighbourhood. Extra lookouts had been posted, the gun crews (the ship carried a four-inch stern gun and four 20mm. Oerlikon AA guns) were at emergency action stations and there had been an increased frequency of course-changes.

I had been ordered to renew the foremast yard-arm signal halyards, which would be heavily used when we got into convoy. This involved going aloft harnessed in a bosun's chair to reach the outer halyard blocks at the extremities of the yard-arm, fifty feet above the deck. By about 15.15 hours this sweaty activity was completed and I made my way from the midship accommodation where cadets were housed to the cadets' bathroom on the main deck, aft of the boat deck, on the starboard side butting onto the steel after main deck. I was wearing my working shorts, t-shirt and soft canvas plimsolls, carried a towel and sponge bag and, of course, every crew member's compulsory companion, a life jacket.

The cadets' bathroom was functional, and in no sense luxurious. It was designed to discourage us from spending too much time away from work and studies. It measured barely eight feet by four and, with the heavy teak door closed, was claustrophic. With two cadets in simultaneous occupation it became distinctly overcrowded, hence the age-old custom of 'first-in-lock-the-door'.

With a sigh of relief, I secured the door behind me and relaxed under the shower. I could hear the waves rushing along the water-line and see, through the open porthole, the peaceful, shimmering South Atlantic disturbed only by a slight breeze and our ship's forward motion. I reflected on the increased bridge alert and emergency crew action stations: obviously Captain Thomas had been advised of enemy action not far away.

Without so much as a whisper of warning, there was a violent explosion almost under my feet. I was flung backwards onto the floor, dazed from a blow on the head. Air burst in through the porthole, bringing with it salt spray and dense, pungent fumes, which filled my small space and made breathing almost impossible. With the ship listing to starboard, I struggled, stumbling and sliding, to regain my footing on the slippery floor. Where was my life-jacket? Blinded by dense smoke, and choking from the fumes, I searched desperately for it. In no time at all the ship's list had increased to 40°. If I did not get out at once, I was going to die, entombed within the small steel bulkheads of the cadets' bathroom.

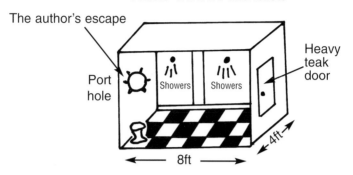

Cadets' showers and toilets

The author's escape

Port hole

Showers Showers

Heavy teak door

4ft

8ft

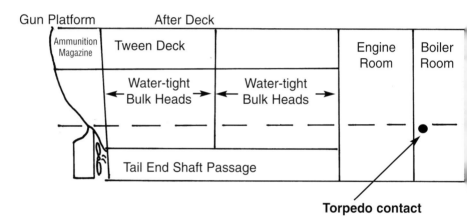

Gun Platform

After Deck

Ammunition Magazine

Tween Deck

Engine Room

Boiler Room

Water-tight Bulk Heads

Water-tight Bulk Heads

Tail End Shaft Passage

Torpedo contact

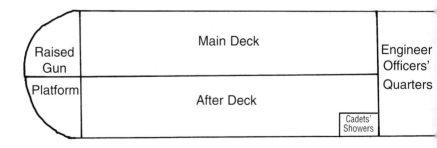

Raised Gun

Main Deck

Engineer Officers'

Platform

After Deck

Quarters

Cadets' Showers

Cadets' Half Deck

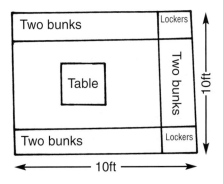

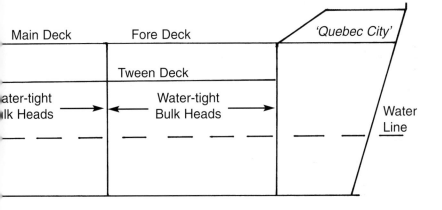

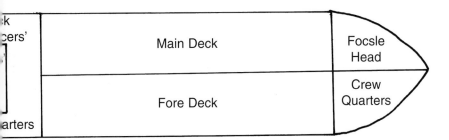

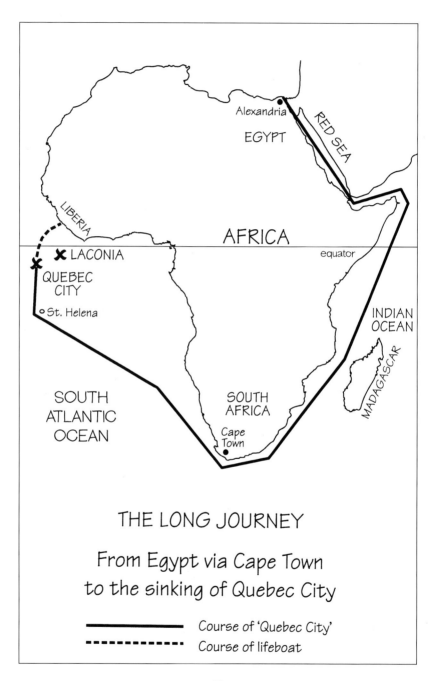

THE LONG JOURNEY

From Egypt via Cape Town
to the sinking of Quebec City

————————	Course of 'Quebec City'
- - - - - - - - - -	Course of lifeboat

CHAPTER ONE

I have often been asked how I came to take up a seafaring career. It's a good question, because I was probably the first member of my family to do so. My mother, however, used to say that a distant relation of ours had run away to sea in 1850, at the age of 15, and become a deck boy in sail. He eventually achieved command, so she believed, of a full square-rigged ocean trader, settled in Liverpool and visited the village of his birth at least once as an affluent gentleman sporting a gold watch and chain. But this had no influence on me, for I did not hear the story until after I had made my own decision.

My mother and father and their forebears were of Cardiganshire farming stock. To the west of the market and university town of Lampeter, two tributaries, the Terwyn and the Cledlyn, meander down to the Teifi, marking the boundaries of where my ancestors farmed. My elder brother was christened Terwyn, after one of them, and my second name, by which I have always been known in the family, is taken from the other.

Ours was a religious family, and as children we were regular attenders at chapel and Sunday School. Although we had no direct opportunities to travel to far-off countries, we did learn about them indirectly because missionaries used to return regularly to their parent chapels to report on their activities. In 1931 or thereabouts, when I was seven years of age, our minister escorted into our Sunday School a man six feet tall, dressed in a flowing silk gown and wearing a circular black Chinese cap with a bobble on top. Our Sunday School teacher and most respected friend, Mr Emrys Walters, had briefed us in advance, but we were spellbound at the sight and fascinated to hear about life in a Chinese village. Always thereafter my mind dwelt on far-off countries and strange lands.

I attended a private day-college, where I was very happy and took an active part in sports, rugby in particular. During my summer holidays I enjoyed country life and got up to all the usual kinds of mischief with the children from neighbouring farms. We went fishing with bent pins for hooks and earthworms as bait or tried to snare trout with nooses made from horsehair. The technique was to find a fish hiding under a stone, hang out the noose in front of its nose and then, by tickling its tail, induce it to move forward into the snare.

Haymaking was a favourite summer activity. Each farmer could count on the help of his neighbours to hand-scythe the crop. We would be out in the fields at dawn and work through to sunset, pausing only for breaks at lunch and teatime, when food was brought to us by the farmers' wives. *Llâth enwyn* (buttermilk) was the popular thirst-quencher during the heat of summer. When the hay had dried, again everyone co-operated to load it into the open-topped horse-drawn carts to carry it to the barns for winter storage. My favourite position was on top of the cart, receiving and stacking the hay as it was lifted up on the eight-foot-long wooden-handled forks. After all had been safely gathered in, we were rewarded with day-trips to Aberaeron or Aberystwyth.

When I was about ten years of age I was invited, together with other children who had helped collect money for the Overseas Missionary Fund, to visit the missionary ship, *John Williams IV*, a beautiful barquentine sailing-ship, berthed at Swansea dock. It had recently returned from the Pacific and was touring the major British ports to raise funds. We were assembled around the large teak ship's wheel, with its bright brass inlays, and told of its voyages in the South Pacific Ocean among exotic tropical islands. My young mind was inspired to wonder how so small a vessel could survive rough seas and high winds and I began to have dreams of taking my own ship to far-off lands and meeting their inhabitants.

By the time I reached the age of fifteen I had applied for the position of Cadet Officer, been accepted and signed all the relevant documents. But by now it was 1939, and on September 2nd, at 11 a.m., Mr Neville Chamberlain announced that our country was in a state of war with Germany. On this historic Sunday morning I was attending morning service at my local chapel with my mother, my brother and my two sisters. When the minister announced that war had been declared, my mother looked at me and shook her head. My nautical career had certainly not been planned to coincide with a world war, but everywhere all males aged eighteen and over were being directed to register for military service. On Monday 3 September a telegram arrived telling me to proceed to Newport docks to join the *Quebec City* on Wednesday 5 September and my mother had to take a hard decision. Should I accept the offer and begin my cadetship, or reject it and wait to be drafted for military service in three years' time?

She was by now a widow, and this made it even more difficult for her to allow her youngest son to go away on active war service. Luckily my godfather, Mr Orllwyn Rees, had been an active and supportive influence ever since the death of my father. I respected him as a father-figure and he and his family treated me as a son. He supported my earnest wish to go to sea, and he was a guiding light to my mother, helping her to agree to my departure. I have never ceased to admire her courage and selflessness and have never forgotten how, forty-eight hours later, when we said our goodbyes, she stood with tears in her eyes, wishing me success and a safe voyage and adding, a typically maternal comment, 'Be a good boy, now!'

Twelve hours later we sailed out of Newport. As we passed Swansea, and I saw the Mumbles light flashing, a heavy weight of homesickness and fear fell upon me. My desire for adventure was overshadowed by the reality of war. But we steamed on at full speed into the dark Atlantic to confront whatever unknown dangers lurked on or under its waves and soon I was too busy filling sandbags and stacking them around the wheelhouse and chartroom against air attack to indulge in personal worries.

War or no war, the life of a cadet was a combination of serious academic study and practical seamanship. I had embarked on my chosen career, and if I was to succeed in it I had to apply myself. It was not easy to adapt to shipboard discipline, but one did not have any choice in the matter. We did our duties and, off duty, we studied – but we had at all times to be ready to man the guns against enemy attack. Often attacks by dive-bombers and U-boats left us little time, but we persevered with physics, spherical trigonometry, calculus, naval architecture and navigation by the sun and stars. All we cadets were well aware that we had to master these subjects in preparation for the major shore examination administered by the Board of Trade. There were six of us cadets aboard the *Quebec City*: two eventually achieved command; one transferred to the South African Airforce as a fighter pilot and three were lost, presumed drowned, as a result of enemy action.

Early in 1940 my ship was fitted with defensive armament: a four-inch Mark 5 stern-gun and four 20mm. Oerlikon single Mark 7A anti-aircraft guns, one each side of the bridge deck and two on the boat deck. The stern had to be strengthened to receive its gun, and magazine spaces constructed for shells and ammunition. There were ready-use shell-racks on the outer radius of the gun-platform and steel lockers for the storage of the cordite charges in their heavy leather containers. In action, these containers were carried on his shoulder by the 'cordite man' whose station was close to the breach, ready to insert the charge behind the shell. This was my position, dangerous because it was so close to the recoil of the gun, and so noisy that I now suffer partial deafness.

Three experienced gunners, Royal Navy long-service men from R.N. Portsmouth, were allocated to us to maintain the guns and to teach our gun-crews naval procedure. We did not take our armament very seriously at first, but a very little convoy experience changed our attitude completely. After relentless hours of drill and practice firing we achieved a good standard, but had the enemy been aware that two thirds of our gun crew comprised cadets aged 15-17, he would surely have been unimpressed. It was more than a year before we were able to attend proper naval base courses, first at the Suez Canal Salt Lakes base, then at R.N. Alexandria where we were given ack-ack practice in the 'dome', firing ball-bearings at a rapidly moving projection of attacking aircraft.

The years 1940 and 1941 were difficult. We spent them on the North Atlantic convoys transporting vital cargoes from the U.S.A. and Canada to the U.K. We were lucky enough to make fourteen crossings unscathed during this period of maximum success for the U-boats, when they sank twelve million tons of shipping.

I recall in particular a voyage to New Orleans to load a full cargo of grain at a time when the U.S.A. was still neutral. All guns had to be dismantled or hidden from view: the Oerlikons were light enough to be unshipped and stowed in the ammunition magazine; the stern gun was covered overall with tarpaulin. We arrived on the Mississippi during the Mardi Gras celebrations and berthed at the foot of Canal Street, near the famous steps where the stern-wheel paddle-steamers board passengers for river cruises.

Local papers made much of our arrival, highlighting the dangers of our voyage across the U-boat-infested Atlantic and the fact that we carried a large gun. Many of the tourists who had flocked in for carnival week came to the Canal Street steps to view this heavily-armed vessel. Dressed in my tropical whites, I had been on gangway duty since 20.00 hours when my shore-leave ended and I had to abandon the delights of the carnival. I was besieged by sightseers begging to be allowed aboard to view the gun – forbidden, of course – and was obliged to work hard to divert their attention with stories about the crossing.

We shipped our cargo of grain, sailed for Halifax, Nova Scotia, to join our eastbound convoy to the U.K., and anchored in Bedford Basin to await final sailing orders. This particular convoy comprised thirty-eight ships, eighteen of which were sunk by U-boat packs operating in severe North Atlantic weather conditions. It was one of the roughest and toughest of the Atlantic convoys and many lives were lost. We considered ourselves lucky indeed to reach Liverpool Bay unharmed.

We proceeded by the ship canal to Manchester, where our cargo was quickly sucked from the holds and stowed safely in the enormous silos which towered over the quayside. We were to sail the next morning, but that very night, with our guns silent because we were not linked to local A.A. control, the *Luftwaffe* began its blitz of the port and city of Manchester. The flour-mills and the silos received direct hits; one silo collapsed directly across our foredeck and the whole of the cargo safely delivered after a 14,000-mile voyage during which we had fought the enemy and the elements was ruined. It rose in enormous pyramids from the murky waters of the dock, a monument to the lost lives of countless seamen.

By December 1941, I was pretty well seasoned in practical, academic and military matters. We sailed from Tilbury for New York via Loch Ewe in the west of Scotland for a westbound North Atlantic convoy. We were due to arrive at New York in early February 1942 to load military supplies (heavily armoured tanks, artillery, small arms and ammunition) for the build-up to the Eighth Army's El-Alamein offensive in North Africa. Before departing Tilbury we received a helium-filled barrage-balloon, which was flown two hundred feet above the mainmast to deter low-level bombing. We sailed in convoy via the North Sea, a highly dangerous area with its 'friendly' minefields, mines laid secretly by enemy aircraft and with hostile airfields in occupied Belgium, Holland and France only a few minutes away.

We reached Loch Ewe safely and it took some thirty-six hours of manoeuvring to get each vessel into its allotted position before the commodore could give the signal to proceed westwards in formation and at the predetermined speed. All signals concerning course and speed were conveyed by flag from the commodore ship and repeated by each ship down the line as acknowledgement. Urgent messages were transmitted in daylight by aldis lamp. After sunset strict blackout was observed: no signals, no smoking on deck or bridge watches. All portholes were closed before sunset; all glass was permanently painted black. Ships proceeded with lifeboats swung out and secured in launching position, a dangerous procedure in the North Atlantic where high running seas with waves up to thirty or forty feet high would lift many a weather-side boat, unhook it from its davits and smash it onto the boat-deck or against the hull. My own ship lost a boat in this way.

Adverse weather caused enormous strain for all officers attempting to maintain close formation with the columns of ships rolling, pitching, pounding and constantly having to adjust their speed. It was not unusual for a convoy encountering really heavy weather to be ordered to disperse and proceed individually until the weather moderated, when a rendezvous position would be given, the escort vessels would round up stragglers and it could take as long as two days to re-form. Our convoy was attacked many times by U-boat packs hunting on the surface at night between the columns. This was a new tactic, and escorting destroyers had great difficulty locating them. During one of these attacks we suffered damage to our stern tube plates when one of our escorts dropped depth-charges too close to us. We were obliged to reduce speed, drop out of the convoy and head for New York unescorted, zig-zagging to confuse the enemy. Eventually, at reduced speed, we made New York. The Ambrose Light Vessel was a welcome sight indeed as we limped into port, passed the Statue of Liberty and anchored to await clearance and orders to proceed to dry-dock on Staten Island.

This was my first visit to the great city and port of New York, a sight and experience never to be forgotten. It radiated greatness and wealth, from the Manhattan skyline's innumerable skyscrapers, reaching upward into the clouds, to the Hudson River at their feet with its hundreds of protruding piers, busy handling ocean liners or waiting for vessels to arrive.

The river swarmed with river-boats; tugs were pushing, towing, nudging craft from large liners to lighters and barges carrying the daily tons of refuse from Manhattan for disposal in landfills on Staten

Island. Threading their way through the crowded river traffic were the large, fast ferries which conveyed the daily crowds of commuters from New Jersey, Brooklyn and Staten Island to Manhattan.

Outstanding above all this maritime hustle and bustle was the calm and graceful Statue of Liberty, looking outward and downward on the prosperous scene. Below it, the once infamous Ellis Island where all immigrants had to pass a searching medical examination and close interrogation before gaining a landing permit. The Statue of Liberty was overwhelming: its foundation alone towered 154 feet over the Parkland, with the gigantic figure rising a further 151 feet. We went inside, re-appearing in due course 300 feet up to walk across the crown of its head for a magnificent panoramic view of the open Atlantic Ocean. For the millions of excited immigrants who sighted it, the Statue of Liberty was a hospitable figure holding out the promise of freedom and a new life in the land of opportunity. This idea of the statue as 'Mother of Exiles' is expressed in a famous poem, 'The New Colossus', written in 1883 by the American poet, Emma Lazarus.

The poem, inscribed on the bronze plaque in the pedestal of the monument in 1903, reads:

> Not like the brazen giant of Greek fame,
> With conquering limbs astride from land to land;
> Here at our sea-washed, sunset gates shall stand
> A mighty woman with a torch, whose flame
> Is the imprisoned lightning, and her name
> Mother of Exiles. From her beacon-hand
> Glows world-wide welcome; her mild eyes command
> The air-bridged harbor that twin cities frame.
> 'Keep, ancient lands, your storied pomp!' cries she
> With silent lips. 'Give me your tired, your poor,
> Your huddled masses yearning to breath free,
> The wretched refuse of your teeming shore.
> Send these, the homeless, tempest-tost to me.
> I lift my lamp beside the golden door!

Our captain, William Caradog Thomas of Amlwch, Anglesey, was forty-eight years of age, Welsh-speaking and a Congregationalist. He was invariably considerate of his crew, officers and men equally, for he had come up through the ranks after beginning his career at the age of fourteen as a deckhand in sail out of Liverpool. He took a fatherly attitude to his cadets, especially when the ship berthed at a major port. Senior cadets (18 or over) were permitted evening shore leave; juniors, like myself, were given afternoon leave with orders to report to the officer of the watch by 20.00 hours.

On the first Saturday, Captain Thomas passed orders to the cadets' half deck that all cadets must be in full uniform and bridge-coats by 08.00 on Sunday in readiness to proceed with him to Manhattan. Unknown to anyone on board, he had arranged for us to attend morning worship at the New York Welsh Congregational Chapel. And he had further arranged that families with teenage children should invite us to spend a few days at their homes as a break from life on board while our ship was drydocked. We received a wholehearted welcome as we marched down the aisle to take our places near the *Sêt Fawr*, the deacons'seat, and Captain Thomas considered our turn-out a credit to his ship and his command. The family with whom I stayed originated from Cwm Rhondda and their daughter was chapel-organist. I spent a very happy five days with them and was given a right-royal tour of New York City.

My first visit was to the Empire State Building, then the highest building in the world. There I had my first (and second) express elevator ride: two were necessary to reach the top. The view was breathtaking, especially looking down to the piers and waterfront where a French Passenger Liner *Normandie* burned furiously, the victim of sabotage. (That night it capsized—a casualty of war—from the tons of water which had been pumped into it to extinguish fire which raged out of control). We also visited the live theatre on Broadway to see Fred Astaire and Ginger Rogers dance their wonderful routine through a musical.

There were two other phenomena, I remember, which spelled America for me: the exceptional aroma of roasting coffee-beans in restaurants, cafes, underground railways, offices and river ferries (it was difficult to order a cup of tea anywhere) and the abundance of smoking everywhere, fanned by large billboards advertising 'Lucky Strike'. Cigars were no less popular and very cheap. The longshoreman would puff away all day on a cigar, whilst the average British citizen could partake in such a luxury, if at all, only at Christmas time. I quickly became addicted to ice-cold chocolate milk and a candy bar named 'Babe Ruth' after the famous Baseball player.

Both these items were available for five cents from a small van with block ice acting as a refrigerator. The van would visit the ships twice daily to sell various favourite fast foods, featuring the 'hot dog'.

As soon as the *Quebec City* was fit for sea, we were loaded to the gunwales with military equipment, which included a deck cargo of a large harbour tug counterbalanced on the port side by three Sherman tanks. We slipped quietly out of New York, alone and unescorted, and were fortunate to make passage safely to Alexandria, Egypt, by way of the bunkering ports at Trinidad and Cape Town. From May 1942 until 6 August we were engaged in shipping supplies to Tobruk and Benghazi.

On 6 August, fully laden with our cargo of Egyptian cotton, we set out on the long voyage home. We proceeded independently and under strict radio silence – U-boats were active in the Indian Ocean – and reached Cape Town, our final bunkering port, in safety. Here we were given shore-leave – highly necessary after our long period at constant action stations in the eastern Mediterranean. Shopping was our main goal, fresh fruit for our own consumption (oranges were coated with wax to preserve them) and presents for our families. I bought a pair of expensive Bata shoes to wear with my blazer when on leave.

Four cadets in the gun crew, Indian Ocean, August 1942.
The author is holding the ramrod.

21

R.N. gun crew colleagues, August 1942.

Three cadets. Author in centre.

We departed Cape Town on the afternoon of 6 September and anchored in Table Bay. Under cover of darkness we weighed anchor and moved out into the U-boat-infested South Atlantic, bound for Freetown where we would join an escorted convoy. Prior to weighing anchor Captain Thomas had received sealed orders from the harbour control naval launch; they contained routeing instructions for independent passage to Freetown, zig-zagging, and passing to the Eastward of St Helena and the Ascension Isles. With the lights of Cape Town fading astern we began our course north-westwards.

Sailors regard the South Atlantic, in normal circumstances, as a friendly ocean. Barking sea-lions escorted us noisily for a whole day and the dolphins soon picked us up on their sonar and raced ahead, playing intricately under the bow-wave. The graceful giant Albatross, never seen north of the Equator, kept us company for days on end. We were fully laden down to our Plimsoll Line, low enough in the water for flying fish to land aboard and add a welcome fresh item to the ship's menu.

Life settled into the standard routine of watch-keeping, navigation and, in my case, allotted day-work (part of my studies) in seamanship; senior cadets were on bridge watch and navigational duties (at which I had taken my turn during our passage of the Indian Ocean). Action stations were frequent, keeping everyone on his toes, the gun-crews going through routine loading-practice on the stern gun. It was my job to place the cordite charge behind the shell; I had to stand so close to the breech in readiness for re-loading that the gunfire deafened me. In the event of air-attack I was gunner on the port boat deck Oerlikon, an anti-aircraft weapon which fired thirty rounds per magazine per minute. Life-jackets lay alongside us at all times and some men had emergency packs containing identity papers, extra clothing and personal items such as letters and photographs of loved ones.

The cadets' half deck accommodation was situated amidships, two decks below the bridge, and comprised six bunks, a table, benches and a (very) well scrubbed teak deck. Two South African cadets, who had served on the naval training ship H.M.S.A. *General Botha*, had left us at Cape Town to prepare for their final examination after completing four years actual sea service. If successful, they would put up a first gold stripe as young qualified officers. Four of us remained, grateful for the extra space which enabled us to move our trunks into the accommodation. These contained all our worldly goods: blazers and grey flannels for civilian wear and tropical uniform, both black and white, heavy weather gear, sea-boots and working clothes. Have-trunk-will-travel was the popular cadet slogan.

Homeward bound after ten months away, we were all in a state of excitement, looking forward to extended home leave and the possibility of transfer to a new ship. Our hopes were scuppered, however, when the captain received revised orders to alter course and to pass to the west of St Helena and the Ascension Islands because of a heavy concentration of U-boats to the east. Lookout activity was intensified, especially in those most dangerous periods, so much favoured by foxy German captains, just prior to sunrise and sunset. The sharpest possible watch was kept to detect the white feather-trail of a periscope or the distant silhouette near the horizon of a U-boat stalking us on the surface.

We sighted St Helena some twenty miles to our starboard beam, partially obscured by heavy rainclouds. So near, and yet so far away. The happy homeward-bound atmosphere had changed to tense apprehension. Were there U-boats lying in wait between us and Freetown? How many? Our radio operators were picking up SOS signals from various allied vessels in trouble, torpedoed and abandoning to the north and east of us. There was nothing to be done but push ahead at full speed and hope to reach the safety of RAF air cover out of Freetown before being attacked.

Saturday 19 September. 15.46 hours. Latitude 2° 12′ South, Longitude 17° 36′ West.

CHAPTER TWO

A torpedo had struck the boiler room area, tearing a huge hole in the steel plating and sending a cascade of water as high as the boat deck. Water rushed into the ship so rapidly that the stokers had no chance to close the hand-operated watertight doors from the engine room side, and very soon the engine room was flooding and the ship began listing heavily to starboard.

I was groping and slithering in the smoke and fumes of the bathroom, but gradually my head cleared and I managed to find my life-jacket and fumble into it. I groped for the door, and located it, but a few moments of frantic tugging revealed that it had been warped and twisted by the explosion and was irretrievably jammed. But the smoke had begun to clear and the light circle of the porthole appeared faintly through its darkness. This was my last and only hope.

Thrusting my head out, I took some deep breaths of clearer air and registered that we were listing so heavily that the sea was running along the main deck starboard scupperways as the ship's continued forward momentum drove it on. The torpedo had struck just forward of the bathroom. Terrified, I hesitated for what seemed like hours before turning to the porthole. It would be impossible to get through with the life-jacket on and fatal to leave it behind, so, having taken it off I held it tightly in one hand, turned my back and began to wriggle out feet-first. My shoulders jammed, but by inching forward and easing one arm through, while the other, still clinging to the life-jacket, remained inside, and then continuing backwards I was able to get my head and then the other arm and the life-jacket safely through. I drew a very deep breath indeed and hurriedly replaced the life-jacket.

Apart from the latter, I was stark naked. I was also soaking wet and shivering even though the air was not cold. Was there time to get back to the half deck for some clothing? There was not: even as the thought was passing through my head the steam whistle began sounding the eight quick short blasts which signified Abandon Ship. With the rest of the survivors I rushed to my lifeboat emergency station on the boat deck. As the final blast died away, an extraordinary silence fell. The main engines had stopped and all that could be heard was the hiss of escaping steam. Few words were exchanged. We stared out over the sea, expecting, at any moment, a second torpedo explosion that would finish us off along with that of the ship. There was no sign of our attacker.

I was standing by the port lifeboat with the heavy, waterproof yellow box – one of my responsibilities was to see that the hand-generated radio transmitter which it contained was taken safely aboard. The order to launch had already been given. The lifeboat was hanging half-way down the side of the heavily listing vessel; I could hear its hull scraping on the shell plating as it inched jerkily down on the hand-controlled rope falls. The yellow box was taken from me, a line bent to it, and it was lowered, ahead of the lifeboat, into the sea and secured.

The seamanlike procedure for launching a lifeboat is that two members of the crew, in this case myself and my dear friend, Michael, a senior cadet, descend with it to unhook the tackle-blocks once it is safely afloat. The boat is first secured by the forward painter, then the tackle-blocks are disconnected from the bow and stern lifting-hooks before the officer in charge on the boat deck gives the order to board. This is accomplished by swarming down knotted rope lifelines. Procedures do not, however, necessarily work smoothly in a real emergency.

U-156 fore-deck gun crew which fired 76 shells into *Quebec City*.

26

Before it became waterborne, I was ordered to take up my position in the now precariously hanging lifeboat. I lowered myself down, hand over hand, by one of the knotted rope lines, feeling it scrape roughly on my bare skin, and pursued by a number of unseamanlike observations from those of my shipmates who had noticed my embarrassment. I had no time to blush. As I reached the bow section, I realised that I was alone. A volley of contradictory orders was shouted. When I shouted back for clarification, it was a long time coming. There was no sign of Michael.

Securing the yellow box was my first priority, and with nobody to help me get it aboard there was a considerable risk that it would be lost. I lowered myself into the sea, holding tightly to the grab-lines with one hand and to the yellow box with the other. Only then did I realise that the ship still had forward momentum: I could see a small bow-wave on the lifeboat's stem and feel the pressure of the water against my shoulders. At this moment one of the three radio officers on the deck thirty-five feet above cast off the line, mistakenly believing that I had the transmitter secure. I clung on desperately, but the pressure of water against my body, lifejacket and, now, the unwieldy transmitter, became too much. My arms felt as if they were being torn from their sockets and I was obliged to release the transmitter in order to save myself. If I had lost my hold and floated away the chances of my being seen from sea-level, let alone rescued, were very slight indeed: the sea is vast and one floating body practically invisible, even from the deck of a ship.

I scrambled back into the lifeboat. Looking up, I could read the dismay on the faces of my shipmates as they watched the yellow box float away astern. Its loss could mean death: we would now have no means of making contact with the outside world and our ship's radio station had failed to transmit an SOS. It would be a long time before anyone came looking for us too. Until we became significantly overdue, Freetown would assume that we were maintaining radio silence as our sailing orders required.

Meanwhile, the launching of the starboard lifeboat had gone seriously wrong when its after fall became unhooked and it was left hanging by its forward fall alone. Unless this could be put right and the lifeboat safely launched, half of the crew had no hope of survival. The captain gave orders that it be lowered to the sea by the one surviving fall and then released onto an even keel. After very strenuous efforts, this was done; but by the time the lifeboat had been released it was full to the gunwales, waterlogged, and there was no one aboard to insert the cork plug into the bung. What's more, members of the crew involved in the struggle had suffered first degree rope-burns which would require urgent medical treatment and pain-killing drugs. Meanwhile the lifeboat was drifting away astern, unmanned.

The *Quebec City*, however, was recovering her equilibrium. The starboard list had reduced by some 15°. No further torpedo had been launched, and there was still no sign of an enemy submarine. As there was no immediate danger of the ship's sinking, the captain ordered that the waterlogged lifeboat be recovered, and other crew members were sent down to join me in the port lifeboat. Among these I was happy to see Michael. An elderly seaman unfortunately lost his hold and fell, striking his head against the steel hull and dropping unconscious into the sea. At this point Michael, without hesitation, went to his rescue. After a struggle, he managed to bring him to the side of the lifeboat so that he could be hauled aboard. Sadly this heroic action proved in vain, for later he died in my friend's arms.

While the captain and the rest of the crew remained on the ship's stern, we had a two-mile row. When we reached the starboard boat we found it full of water and with various essential items of equipment floating free, but luckily nothing had been lost overboard. We baled out the lifeboat and made it seaworthy and inhabitable. We then rowed both lifeboats back to the ship, very surprised to find her now floating upright and still. Two and a half hours had passed since the explosion, and still there was no sign of further enemy action. Orders were given for the release of the two emergency rafts from their positions on the port and starboard rigging, and we recovered from them their stores, fresh-water tanks and items such as rope and canvas which would be useful on our imminent voyage.

Everyone except the captain then boarded a lifeboat. He remained aboard the *Quebec City*, a lonely, sad figure on a silent ship. As she showed no sign of sinking, we began to think of re-boarding, but then he shouted that he had sighted a periscope five hundred yards off the port beam. We were all extremely apprehensive at this, for we had heard propaganda accounts of the barbarities of Nazi captains who had machine-gunned ships' boats and survivors swimming for their lives. Was this captain enjoying a cat-and-mouse game with us? Had he now tired of it and decided on the kill? One short burst of automatic fire would be enough to finish us.

Captain Thomas lowered the white, duck-canvas, lead-weighted bag which contained the naval secret deciphering books and our routeing orders which it was his duty to destroy to prevent them from falling into enemy hands. He climbed down the Jacob's ladder and took command, issuing immediate instructions that if the U-boat surfaced, he, and he alone would respond to any questions put by its commander. We rowed away from the lee of our ship and waited, resting on our oars, for what fate had determined for us.

We could all see the periscope now, moving towards us very slowly. The sea was calm, and so crystal clear that we were able to see the U-boat's hull as it passed slowly by. The periscope was no more than two feet away – I could have reached out and touched it. We could see the forward gun, the conning-tower, just breaking surface, almost awash, and a lighter gun abaft the conning-tower. We braced ourselves, sure now that it was about to surface directly underneath, capsize the boats and throw us all into the sea. But it passed us by without incident. Sure now that the submarine would shortly surface, the captain jettisoned the canvas weighted bag. Those officers whose white shirts bore epaulettes indicating their rank tore them off, having heard reports of senior officers being taken aboard U-boats as prisoners of war. Being still entirely naked apart from a life-jacket, I had no such problem!

We realised that the commander of the U-boat was not playing any cat-and-mouse game with us, merely being very cautious. The stern gun of the *Quebec City* was twice the size of any armament carried by his vessel, and he may well have suspected that our Captain and crew, assembled on the stern, were waiting for the chance of a shot at him when he surfaced. It was a further quarter of an hour before he had satisfied himself that nobody remained on board and he could now safely surface.

I was sitting next to a young junior ordinary seaman from Anglesey. Cadets were not permitted to fraternize aboard ship, or to invite any crew member to visit the half deck, but he and I had become good friends when working together on deck and learning the rudiments of seamanship. As the U-boat reached the surface and moved towards us, he slipped his hand into mine and grasped it tightly. He, too, had heard more than enough stories of atrocity.

We are ordered alongside U-156.

The U-boat's crew were taking up action stations at the fore and after guns. Half-way up the conning-tower was a circular catwalk on which stood six men, smartly uniformed in green khaki battledress and forage caps. Each of them carried an automatic quick-firing machine gun pointed in our direction. On top of the conning-tower stood the submarine's commander and some of his senior officers, also smartly turned out in green khaki battledress. The commander was easily distinguishable by his cap with its gold-braided peak. He was a tall, military figure and on either side of him was a lookout ceaselessly scanning sea and sky through powerful binoculars. They spared us not a glance: their vigilance meant life or death to their vessel – a U-boat on the surface was very vulnerable to air attack.

The enemy commander now ordered us, in clear, well-pronounced English, to come alongside and as soon as we had done so we were made fast. To our surprise, we received a friendly greeting from our captors. These men showed none of the arrogance we had expected; we felt that if we remained calm we were going to survive. We studied the U-boat with great interest. It was much bigger than I had expected – over 250 feet long – and appeared to be in pristine condition, with no evidence of fouling by barnacles or sea-grass. It was painted a deep grey-green and the only distinguishing mark it bore was a coloured crest, a coat of arms, on the conning-tower.

A tense silence fell, broken only by the steady throbbing of the submarine's compressors. Then our captain was asked to identify himself. Captain Thomas stood up in the lifeboat's stern and gave his rank, whereupon he received an apology for the torpedoing of his ship. War was war, alas! he was told, and it was the duty of each of us to serve his flag and country. Standard questions were asked: ship's name, tonnage, flag, where from, where bound, what cargo.

Then the German seemed to relax. He said that it would have been his wish to tow our lifeboats at least some of the distance between us and the African coast. He regretted, however, that he was not able to give such assistance as he had recently been attacked while on the surface attempting to save survivors' lives. He asked whether we did intend to make for the African mainland or to head south instead, for the Ascension Islands, which were much closer. While it was true that the nearest part of the African coast, Cape Palmas on the southernmost tip of Liberia, was about 1,200 miles away, the Ascension Islands were very small in the vast expanse of the South

Atlantic, our sea-level horizon was at best five miles distant and with just one spirit-floating compass, the risk of failing to make landfall in that direction was very great.

Captain Thomas said that we would head for Africa, and his German colleague fully agreed and invited him on board the U-boat to study his charts and confirm our position relative to Cape Palmas. The only serious danger was that the strong prevailing south-easterly currents which sweep down the West African coast could carry us south of Cape Palmas and into the Gulf of Benin, which extends a further thousand miles to the coast of Nigeria and the Cameroons. The Ascension Islands, however, apart from being a small target for an open boat, are often shrouded by mist, and if we missed them we might well have ended up in Antarctica.

In spite of the German commander's concern about our well-being, he did not inquire about our provisions (by no means adequate for the jouney that lay before us), nor did he offer us additional food or water. He was, of course, much further from a friendly coast than we were, and no doubt had his own anxieties about food, fuel, and making a rendezvous with his 'milch-cow'. He wished us good luck and expressed the hope that we might meet in the future under better circumstances, in a world of non-aggression. As I sat there in silence, trying to come to terms with the situation, I reflected that this man and his crew appeared not to be Nazis, but genuine German naval officers and ratings operating in accordance with the Geneva Convention. There had been no sign of hatred or bigotry, only that mutual respect and comradeship which is normal between true seamen, who feel an instinctive duty to assist one another in difficulties, irrespective of peace or war.

We were now ordered to move off and keep well clear of our crippled ship – which, however, showed no sign of sinking – as the U-boat intended to finish it off with shellfire. The order was given to cast off. We heard the pop-pop-pop of the diesels. The German rating nearest me said, quietly, as he let go our line and cast it towards me, 'Good luck,' and I replied, 'Thank you.'

U156 moved slowly around the *Quebec City*'s stern, gun crews preparing both the fore and after guns for action. We rowed our lifeboats into a position well astern so as to observe the shelling from a safe distance and to be clear of suction when the vessel sank. U156 stood off some 250 yards on the starboard beam, amidships, and commenced firing shells into her hull along the waterline. We could see the shells explode on impact, but the old warhorse remained upright and unmoved. She was withstanding everything her enemy could throw at her.

The initial torpedo had damaged but failed to sink her. The shelling seemed futile. The stern was targeted, and fire broke out there. At last a direct hit on the magazine caused a huge explosion in the transom and the stern began to settle and the bow to rise.

A heavy depression settled over the lifeboats. We began to pray that the U-boat might fail to sink her, and to fantasise again about re-boarding. It was deeply humiliating to sit helpless while our companion and home-from-home was put to a lingering death. The lifeboats bobbed up and down in the slight sea; nobody spoke. Each individual cherished his own thoughts. Married men wondered if they would ever see their wives and children again; the younger men thought of parents, brothers and sisters, schoolfriends. We all knew now about the failure to broadcast an S.O.S. and we were all well aware of its implications.

A muffled explosion came from the *Quebec City* as a watertight bulkhead collapsed. The stern and part of the after deck became submerged; the bow was moving towards an upright position. Two further muffled explosions indicated the collapse of two more bulkheads under the weight of the invading sea. The result was hard to credit: the ship literally stood up vertically. Then the last two bulkheads gave way and she slipped, quietly and gracefully, into the depths of the South Atlantic. There was surprisingly little disturbance of the water, only a turbulence of foam and bubbles as the bow disappeared below the surface.

There were tears in many eyes, my own included. The U-boat dived on a westerly course and disappeared. We were alone. 17.10 hours. Latitude 2° 12' South, Longitude 17° 36' West. Saturday 19 September 1942. Three hours had passed since the torpedo struck. It was obvious to all of us that our survival was now dependent on our working as a team for as long as our strength remained.

Captain Thomas ordered the two lifeboats together to discuss tactics and to tend those who had suffered injuries. It took the combined medical supplies of the two boats to give some relief to those with rope-burns, who required morphia tablets under the tongue to ease their pain. Most of the bandages and burn-gauze were used up on the four victims of burns. Those with minor injuries willingly went without treatment. I put forward my left foot for attention – it had been torn from instep to ankle on a jagged steel plate. But the blood had congealed and it was, for the moment, regarded as a minor injury not requiring urgent attention. Our 'medical officer' (the purser) instructed me to wash it daily in salt water.

Our immediate task was to organize ourselves before the rapidly oncoming nightfall. Six-hour watches were arranged, masts stepped and sails hoisted. Our home for the foreseeable future was a twenty-five-foot, clinker-built wooden lifeboat, fifteen years old. My lifeboat was the ship's motor-boat, and had a small Perkins engine and four gallons of petrol – for emergency use only: towing other lifeboats and rafts quickly away from a stricken ship. The captain, who was aboard the second lifeboat with twenty-two men, decided to use the engine to tow his boat until the petrol supply was exhausted. This would have given an effective speed of 3 or 4 knots for a period of 40 hours. But the engineer responsible for the weekly testing and maintenance of the engine confessed that he had found a fault in its magneto, taken the faulty part to his cabin for attention . . . and that it had gone down with the ship.

We had already been deprived of our emergency transmitter, and now our engine was useless. How many more disappointments awaited us? As it was seven hours since we had eaten or drunk, it was decided to issue rations before darkness fell. These had to be calculated on the basis of a voyage lasting twenty days at least, and it was agreed that food and water should be issued three times a day, at 6 a.m., 12 noon and 6 p.m., as follows:

6 a.m.: one hard biscuit, three cubes pemmican (beef extract), two ounces of water.

12 noon: one biscuit, three cubes pemmican, two ounces of water.

6 p.m.: one cube pemmican, two pieces chocolate, two ounces of water, one Horlicks tablet (this proved too rich and made us sick).

Our new home was heavily encrusted with paint from many years of upkeep and a good deal of its space was taken up by the oars, each eight feet long, the useless engine and a large folded canvas lifeboat cover. Twenty men had to find a permanent seat on thwarts or side-benches. The stern was a 'no-go' area reserved for the officer of the watch and his watch-keepers, who took hourly spells steering and tending sail. A lookout was stationed forward, alongside the mast, on hourly watch. Under the wooden side-benches were the copper buoyancy tanks which would keep the boat afloat if, as had been the case with the second boat, it became waterlogged. Beneath the thwarts were the provisions, two tanks of fresh water and two foodstore tanks. At both bow and stern there was locker space for spare ropes and a sea-anchor. The compass was contained in a box binnacle bolted to the after thwart close to the helmsman. There were two knives and axes, in the care of the officer of the watch for safety's sake, three metal bailers and three dippers measured in ounces for the rationing of water. The forward locker was large enough to accommodate two men in a cramped position and, to our surprise, three slim Asian firemen took up residence there on this first night and never emerged – the most we ever saw of them was two hands extended to receive rations for three men.

We relished our water ration after the hot, exhausting, stressful day, and it was decided to keep the two boats together with a tow-line. Under sail, however, this proved entirely unseamanlike: one boat would surge ahead, the line become taut and the second boat would be turned 180°. After an hour or two of this it was reluctantly resolved to cast off the line and proceed independently. We maintained contact in the darkness by shouting words of encouragement to each other.

That first night was very long and extremely uncomfortable. Each of us turned and twisted as he tried to find space in which to stretch out and catch some sleep. Tempers frayed as over-tiredness and the delayed effects of shock affected us. Staring up, half asleep, into the clear equatorial sky, you saw the stars rock slowly back and forth to the rhythm of the boat. The night grew damp and cold and we had only four blankets for twenty-one men. I still had no clothing other than my lifejacket, cold, wet, sodden with salt water. I felt no compunction in sharing a blanket with three able seamen. I understood now the truth of stories I had read of deserts becoming cold after nightfall. Here we were, not far from the Equator, shivering in a light, cool breeze.

Two watches had been formed. I was allotted the 12-6 watch and my friend Michael the 6-12 under Chief Officer Sloane. The officer of my watch was the Shetland Islander third officer, a very seasoned seaman with much experience of fishing off his homeland in his younger days. He was expert in manipulating the sail to the greatest advantage. Our only light was provided by one oil lamp and the small binnacle lamp, but the latter caused so many problems that we were reduced to using a hand-torch to read the compass and steering by the stars. As our engine was useless, we decided to use its small store of petrol to burn a flare every three hours in the hope of attracting the attention of an aeroplane or surface craft.

The simple notion of burning a flare proved more difficult than we had foreseen. What could we use to soak with petrol? The only cloth or waste available was what we were wearing. Someone suggested canvas, so we cut a small piece from the lifeboat cover, set it on the end of the six-foot boathook and ignited it with a cigarette lighter. It flared brightly at first, but by the time the boat-hook reached the vertical position it had sunk to a flicker and immediately thereafter it faded out. Obviously the canvas was both too thick and saturated with sea water.

Sitting in this uncomfortably small, fifteen-year-old wooden life-boat, in a position south-west of the West African bulge of mainland Africa, my thoughts inevitably turned to what my oceanographical and meterological studies had taught me—that this, in mid-September, was a turbulent weather region. Here low-pressure systems form at the equinox, when the sun, directly overhead in a clear blue sky, makes it scorching hot. In this area, during this month, hurricanes are born, of high sea-surface temperatures and favourable upper-level winds which coincide for a brief period. They begin as depressions and move slowly westward, gathering speed and intensity as they approach the land mass of the Windward Islands; in the Caribbean they reach their savage maturity.

It was a most dangerous area for an open boat under sail, subject to weather conditions liable to vary from flat calm to squally, fresh winds up to force 6 accompanied by torrential rain squalls—an unnerving prospect, a grave misfortune.

We continued to maintain contact with the other boat by shouting and whistling, but the response grew fainter and farther away.

CHAPTER THREE

When dawn broke, the light breeze had dropped to a calm, the ocean as far as we could see was glossy and still and our sails hung limp. The whole circle of the horizon was empty of life. Our shipmates were nowhere to be seen. We were alone now.

Weary from lack of sleep, aching from my cramped and awkward position, forlorn, dejected, naked, I rubbed my eyes and considered my future. Was my young life approaching an early end? What chance was there of surviving the sea, the sun, the threat of despair, and coming safe to shore? What unforeseeable hazards lay ahead? We had transmitted no message; our emergency transmitter had floated away; our boat's engine was defective. I took a deep breath and resolved that, come what may, David Cledlyn Jones was going to survive.

At last it was 6 a.m. We sipped our water, making the most of every drop, chewed and mouthed the hard biscuit and pemmican until the last bit of nourishment was extracted. It was not much, but we all brightened up and set to work. The useless engine was dismantled and, apart from such potentially useful items as nuts, bolts and copper pipe, committed to the deep. We gained a small additional amount of elbow-room and some morale-boosting exercise.

The sun approached its midday position vertically overhead and beat down upon us. There was no sign of forward movement, no wake; crabwise, we drifted. To refresh ourselves, we dived into the cool, inviting sea, and my injured left foot enjoyed the salt-water treatment which had been prescribed for it. I stayed in the water for twenty minutes, clinging to the grab-lines. Spirits rose, some of my shipmates, becoming quite boisterous, swam around the boat, climbed back on board and dived off the gunwale again. They were warned, however, to conserve their energy for a long haul.

Our watch was known as 'the singing watch': many of the sailors were from Amlwch on Anglesey. During our second night the weather became squally and it did our hearts good to hear the flow of water along the hull as the boat began to move positively forward. We urged it on with hearty singing, a combination of the sacred and profane: 'Calon Lân' and 'Maggie May'! By about 10 p.m. we were making enough headway to take a little spray on the starboard bow. My enthusiasm was literally damped by this as I struggled, in wet blankets, to snatch a little sleep before my midnight watch duties. Optimism is hard to maintain when you are tired, cannot sleep and have no hot food or drink.

At about 2 a.m. on the third day we were almost overtaken by calamity when our rudder mysteriously became detached, we thought as a result of being struck by some large fish feeding on the surface. Luckily the helmsman was alert and grabbed the rudder before it could float away into the darkness. The top gudgeon pin and its surrounding attachment had been damaged. We were very much alarmed because, without the rudder, we could not maintain course. By the light of torches we assessed the damage, realising immediately that major repairs were necessary. This would require careful thought and considerable ingenuity as soon as it was daylight.

We could not afford to be without steerage for so long, so we shipped an oar through the stern bulwark rowlock and attempted to use its blade as a rudder. Small river craft are frequently steered in this way – it is called 'sculling' – but it is no joke trying to do so with an unwieldy, fully laden, twenty-five-foot lifeboat. The eight-foot oar was extremely ungainly also, but it was just possible, using strength we could ill afford to spend – it required the efforts of two men at a time, and a half-hour shift was as much as we could manage. Ingenuity was required, too, in manoeuvring the main sail and jib. We had to give up steering by compass and use a star low on the horizon.

Dawn and the 6 a.m. change of watch and issue of rations were very welcome when, at last, they arrived. But sunrise usually brought an end to the gentle breezes that blew during darkness and we did not look forward to another long, sweltering day. Struggling with the temporary rudder had exhausted us. Worse, our shipwright was in the other lifeboat, so we had to work out for ourselves how best to manage a repair with the limited materials available. The steel section which secured the upper gudgeon pin was handed over to the engineers while the rest of us set about repairing the wooden portion. The third officer it was who suggested removing the bow and stern locker doors from their hinges, shaping them and bolting them together over the damaged area. It was very fortunate that we had kept the nuts and bolts from the dismantled engine.

For thirty-six hours we struggled alternately with the repair and the brutally awkward steering oar. With knife and axe we shaped the doors.

The engineers contrived makeshift bolts. Tired, struggling to control our irritation, we managed to complete the repair – no small job: the complete rudder was six feet in height and two feet wide. We now attempted to install it. But when the lower gudgeon pin was pushed home, the upper was out of alignment, and vice versa. We gritted our teeth, struggled on, made adjustment after adjustment – and, at last, succeeded. We could return to normal steering and recuperate.

During the endless discussions which accompanied the repair, we agreed that it was not a large fish that had caused the trouble, but old age. The bolts securing the gudgeon pin clamps had rusted, the rust had penetrated the surrounding timber and this had rotted. To celebrate an achievement that undoubtedly saved our lives we were given permission for a swim. But the cool sea was less inviting than it had been to men tired out from the heavy expense of strength on the steering oar. Those who did swim had evident trouble climbing back aboard, and once everyone was safely back the senior officer ruled that it would be unwise to swim in future: all available energy would have to be conserved for shipboard tasks and the possibility of further emergencies.

We were into our fifth day and I noticed that there was a tendency to flare up at the least excuse and that the smokers (fortunately I was not one of them) were particularly irritable. They settled to pool such cigarettes as they had, though many of them were soaked with salt water and unsmokable. When you have little to do, it passes the time to study the behaviour of your fellow men, and it was very interesting to see how the nicotine addicts tried to cope. First they would carefully separate the tobacco from the wet cigarette-paper and spread it out to dry. This they did with great care, turning it frequently and fondling it with affection. When the tobacco was dry, one cigarette would be rolled from it, lit and passed around, only one inhalation per person being permitted. Inevitably, there were those who tried to exceed their ration, and, as time went by and nerves became worse, strong words were exchanged and, sometimes, even blows. The 40-60 per-day men suffered greatly from withdrawal symptoms and as soon as a cigarette was lit you could see them become tense and aggressive as they waited their turn, watching, with accusing, greedy eyes, to make sure that nobody broke the rules.

In spite of our best efforts with the temporary rudder, we had lost many miles during the 36 hours it had taken to make repairs, so we sought ways to improve our sail area. The obvious way was by adding a spinnaker, but would the mast take the extra strain – and what would be our position if it were to snap? After careful discussion it was decided to take a chance. If the mast did snap we had an oar as stout as the mast available for a jury-rig. We had enough canvas, recovered from one of the rafts and, using a spare oar to secure the large spinnaker to the base of the mast, we created an extra area of sail. Larger than the original mainsail, it projected a long way out over the starboard gunwale, giving us something of the air of a far eastern sail tea-clipper in full rig. But the wind died and we lay becalmed all afternoon.

I had continued to soak my damaged foot daily in the sea and, although the wound had become spongy, it was clean to the (visible) bone. While it was tender to touch, it gave no serious pain. I had hoped that it might have closed up by now and wondered if stopping the salt-water treatment might bring this about. But I was afraid that the dirt in the lifeboat might cause infection, so continued to dangle my leg over the side.

With the excitements of the rudder and the spinnaker behind us, the days became monotonous. The only significant events were the issuing of rations, desultory chatting and as much sleep as could be managed when off watch. Conversation grew less from day to day and soon someone asked the inevitable question: how long could we go on like this? This frightened me, for I had been clinging to my confidence that we would either make land before supplies ran out or be rescued by another ship. We could not help being depressed by our slow progress, particularly during daylight hours when the merciless sun burned us out of a clear sky. Salt water, drying and baking all over my body, had made my skin very taut. I tried putting a blanket over my shoulders and, although rough on the skin and uncomfortably hot, it did prevent my back from being scorched.

On the evening of the fifth day, just as everyone had settled down for another uncomfortable night, the sails began gently flapping and ripples began to lap the sides of the boat. Was this the steady breeze we had been praying for? Within the hour our sails were billowing out and we were truly on the move. We estimated that, with the addition of the spinnaker, we were making at least three knots, and this put a smile on every face.

Suddenly we felt rain on our faces, light at first, then developing into a heavy downpour. We sat bolt upright, mouths opened wide, hands cupped to catch water fresh as champagne. It soaked my hair, ran down over my forehead, dripped from my nose and cheeks, filled my gaping, thirsty mouth. It was a brackish champagne at first, from the salt deposits in hair and on skin, but it ran clearer and oh, was it welcome! My whole desiccated being seemed to soften and swell with life. Typically, the rain was turned off like a tap after about twenty minutes, but to our additional delight the wind was not; if anything it increased slightly.

The mast was bearing the strain, and the repaired rudder gave no trouble. Animated conversation returned. It was a pleasure to be soaked from head to foot in fresh water. We realised that we had been so surprised and delighted by the downpour that we had failed to take proper advantage of it – we ought to have had arrangements in place to catch and preserve as much as possible. Hoping for further opportunities, we prepared the old canvas lifeboat-cover which had been stowed in the stern locker: there were tears and holes in it, but large areas remained intact and capable of catching the next shower.

At five o'clock on the morning of day six, after an excellent night's sailing, we saw an area of dark cloud approaching. Rain, surely! All hands set to to spread the canvas cover from mast to stern to make a catchment area. We were ready to scoop the water up with bailers and transfer it to one of the fresh-water tanks: we had two of these, and only one day's supply, two at best, remained in the first of them.

The dark cloud duly delivered a downpour and, by allowing the canvas to sag in the centre, we soon accumulated quite a large quantity of water. After about forty minutes we began baling water into the almost empty tank. But we had recovered no more than four partly-filled bailers when two men, unable to control themselves any longer, threw themselves onto the canvas. It collapsed, spilling all that remained of the water uselessly into the bottom of the boat.

This was the first sign that discipline was starting to break down. It was well that the axes were in the care of the officers of the watch or violence would surely have been done. As it was, it was only with difficulty that we prevented those within reach of the defaulters from seriously harming them. They were severely reprimanded by the chief and the third officer and they both apologised at once and sincerely. They were quite unable to explain their action – but, sadly, we learned later that they had been surreptitiously drinking sea-water.

Such, however, is the life of an open boat that our morale was sharply improved three hours later by the discovery of a small hair-comb under the floorboards. It proved a focus of interest and pleasure, each of us taking his turn to comb his hair and developing beard. The comb was carefully kept alongside the compass binnacle and passed daily from hand to hand after the 6 a.m. issue of rations so that we could groom ourselves to face another day. Apparently trivial things can be the difference between life and death: even though we had not washed for a week or more, our self-respect was maintained.

When the first ration of salvaged rainwater was served, at midday, the first men to try it coughed and spat their two ounces into the sea. It had a foul smell and brackish taste – of salt water, bad eggs and canvas. Our makeshift reservoir had become impregnated with salt spray, dirt and dust over many years. We had to open our last freshwater tank, but anyone who cared to was allowed extra from the contaminated supply. There was no rush for this, but as the sun sank down that evening, two of us decided to try an experiment. We unbolted the tank from the thwart and studied the inside, which appeared quite clean. Floating on top of the water was a crust of algae, which we painstakingly removed: there seemed to have been some kind of reaction between the galvanized lining and the salty water. It was the algae which were producing the foul smell and taste.

Having removed as much of the crust as possible, we recovered a full dipper – six ounces or so – of water and sipped it between almost closed lips so as to exclude any remaining algae, grimacing fiercely as we did so in an attempt to dissuade our comrades from trying it. They were not deceived, and everyone received a supplementary ration – the water was drinkable now, if only just.

Day seven arrived. The weather had returned to its predictable pattern. I continued to dangle my leg over the gunwale for the sake of my wound, and suddenly some joker shouted, 'Shark!' and I had to get it back into the boat in a great hurry while everyone laughed. There were no sharks; in fact, very little marine life of any kind. But coincidentally, that same afternoon, a genuine shark's fin was sighted off the starboard bow and kept us company, at a wary distance, for about half-an-hour – a reminder that there *were* unseen dangers lurking.

Our stamina dwindled. Even small routine tasks such as hauling tight the halyards were an effort. It was difficult to come to terms with sleepless, chilly nights, made worse by the fact that we were seldom dry during the dark hours. If anyone lingered over his two ounces of water – we had only two graduated dippers – he would be cursed by men unable to await their turn in patience. The cigarette-smokers were edgier than ever and there was real hatred in their eyes if they suspected a shipmate of trying to take more than his share. Our nights were made more restless by men with very little in their stomachs retching and gasping. Most of us suffered this, from the contaminated water, we thought. We had abandoned our efforts to refill the tank; each man was now free to collect whatever he could by his own methods when it rained. Those seated forward near the mast and sails could take advantage of rainwater running off the sails, but it was always brackish and no one dared take much of it.

The seventh night was our roughest yet, with squalls up to Force 5 and steering troublesome. With all sails set, the boat was shipping heavy spray, and mast and boat alike creaked ominously. It was exciting, exhilarating and dangerous, the boat driving on at roughly five knots, a remarkable achievement for a twenty-five-foot lifeboat under sail, and a thrilling experience. Our Shetland Islands third officer showed true seamanship that night, personally handling the tiller during the squalls and rapping out decisive orders for the handling of the sails. Six feet tall, powerfully built, with heavily-muscled arms and shoulders, he was an inspiration to us all and we certainly should not have survived without his tireless efforts and determination. The driving rain enabled everyone to get a good share of fresh water. Eventually we were obliged to lower the spinnaker for safety's sake, but we did this reluctantly: maximum speed was becoming increasingly important.

Dawn broke with nobody having enjoyed any sleep at all, but the squalls died away in time for the 6 a.m. ration issue. There was a lot of grumbling about aches, pains and cramp; everybody was soaked through and depressed. The senior officer was repeatedly asked by one or two men where we were, when we would make landfall, was there any real hope of survival. Even whether it was worth continuing. There could be no clear answer to any question but the last, and there the reply of the majority was loud and clear. Uncomfortable we might be, but we were well pleased with the distance we had covered during the night. The moaners were told that we had every intention of coming through and that if they planned to give up they should do it during the hours of darkness so as not to upset the rest of us.

That evening, Mr Moffat, for the benefit mainly of the malcontents, gave a lecture on astronomy. He pointed out the Plough, which was clearly visible low down on the starboard bow and explained how it could be used to locate the Pole Star, just visible at that time above the horizon on the port bow. He explained that we had abandoned ship at two and a half degrees south of the Equator, and that from that position the Pole Star was not visible. We had therefore made significant progress into the North Atlantic and were on course for landfall on the 'Bulge of Africa' (Liberia). This silenced the Doubting Thomases, and we never again heard a squeak out of them.

Michael Hughes and I would pass many a daytime hour remembering our shared experiences. We had sailed together from London, New York, Chittagong in northeast India, battled our way across the Atlantic in various convoys. We particularly remembered our most recent service in the eastern Mediterranean, supporting the Eighth Army. When we reached the U.K. Michael would enter nautical college in London to study for and sit his first examination. Success would mean promotion to third officer on his next appointment. Very quietly, we would discuss also the pros and cons of our present position: as cadets, junior officer rank, we had no authority – but if anything happened to the first or third officer we must be prepared to play our part.

We commiserated with one another about the loss of so many personal possessions – family photographs, watches, pens, clothing (including, in my case, the brand-new shoes that I should never wear) – and about the loss of our papers. At this moment we were, very literally, stateless persons, with no way of proving our identity, no pass book, no food or clothes ration books so essential on home leave. We discussed our prospects of a safe and acceptable landfall; what if we overshot both Liberia and Sierra Leone and came ashore in Vichy territory: Senegal or Dakar? In that case we should be interned for the duration of hostilities, no doubt in highly unpleasant conditions. We discussed this at length with our officers, believing that our course was rather too much north of NNE in our efforts to make sure that we did not overshoot south into the Bight of Benin. It was agreed to adjust course somewhat to the south of NNE, bearing in mind that it was difficult to steer consistently within 15 to 20 degrees of an exact NNE heading.

The ninth day dawned pleasantly: clear sky, rippling sea, a light,

44

warm breeze. The off-watch crew had slept rather well during a quiet night and it was very pleasant not to have to listen to a series of complaints. We enjoyed – as far as this was possible – our breakfast rations, and the smokers managed an uncontentious round of single inhalations. The officers put us to work tidying the boat, baling out the water from under the bottom boards and making everything as far as possible shipshape and Bristol fashion. Everyone became cheerfully involved in this; we even managed to remove one of the Asians from the forward locker space, but the others were so reluctant to be moved that we gave up trying. All remaining provisions were then carefully checked.

We had sufficient rations for approximately seven days: hard biscuits, pemmican, Oxo cubes and chocolate (surprisingly, this remained solid and did not melt away), and we had plenty of Horlicks tablets. There were also four cans of 'Omnopan' tablets, sealed and intact. We had not yet had to resort to these, and they were never referred to: their purpose was to relieve severe depression, and their time might yet come. For the present, although we were all of us depressed from time to time, no one, fortunately, had become clinically so. We had some morphine tablets left also: those who had suffered rope-burns had recovered from the initial severe pain.

Next it was suggested that the medical condition of each one of us should be assessed, for although we knew ourselves how we were feeling, this had never been publicly discussed. Many of my shipmates were embarrassed at having to talk on this subject, but I was long past all embarrassment, having been naked since abandoning ship. Surprisingly, everyone's respiratory organs seemed to be in good order. We assumed that our blood pressure was relatively normal, having no intruments to establish the contrary. As for bowel-movements, only one man had achieved any movement in ten days (he had been brave even to attempt it, straining on the bucket, in full view of twenty men for half an hour to such an extent that he almost collapsed afterwards) – yet we were not suffering from furred tongues or foul-tasting mouths. Urine had been passed normally for the first five days, then its quantity and flow progressively reduced by low water-intake, and its odour increasingly rank. No-one worried greatly about bowel-movement – after all, our intake of solids was virtually nil – but we were deeply concerned about lack of urine, fearing kidney damage.

As far as injuries were concerned, with the exception of my left foot, now giving cause for concern, most had fully healed. My wound remained open and it was becoming painful to put any weight at all on the leg. With only sea-water to cleanse the wound, I was afraid that gangrene might set in. We were all physically weak, of course, and this led to inceasing irritability, the least little thing being capable of causing arguments and strong language. Little things like three men sharing one blanket when they fell asleep and two waking, cold and wet, to find the third, the artful dodger, snugly wrapped up at their expense. On the other hand, nobody was now strong enough to throw a punch capable of doing any damage.

Mentally – apart from the shortness of temper – we appeared entirely normal. Nobody wandered in thought or in speech. Married men with families, however, tended to be withdrawn and distraught: I heard two of them crying one night and they had to be comforted by their neighbours and encouraged to believe that each day was taking us closer to land, survival and return to their loved ones. Younger people, like myself, were still capable of seeing the voyage as adventure, but we probably suffered worse from enforced idleness and monotony. All longed for a sight of land, a passing ship or aircraft. We were sure that by now searches were being made for us and we had a good chance of being found. But every day that passed without so much as the sound, even, of an aircraft, undermined morale.

Early on the morning of the tenth day I was on the tiller, seated next to the officer of the watch. He was carving a tenth notch on the handle of one of the axes. How many more notches, I asked him, did he expect before landfall? He took his time answering, evaluating in his mind the likely mileage covered each day. On the first day, he estimated, we had had eleven hundred miles to make good. He pointed to the Pole Star and reminded me that it had not been visible at all, but now daily appeared higher above the horizon. In a whisper he told me that his best guess, allowing for our past speed in squally weather and the time spent becalmed, was 'possibly four days if we get enough breezes to keep us moving forward.' Cheered by his words, I asked why he was whispering. 'Everyone wakes up in hope each morning,' he said. 'I don't want them waking in four days' time and losing heart because my dead reckoning's a day or two out.'

The information was good enough for me, though. I was cheered and quite excited at the prospect of only four more days of discomfort and uncertainty. After 6 a.m. rations I reported the discussion to Michael and asked him to make a similar approach to the chief officer when he had his next trick at the helm. At midday rations, however, the latter issued a public statement about our progress, emphasising that he and the third officer were of the considered opinion that, if favourable breezes continued, land would probably be sighted within four or five days. Morale rose sharply and bets were laid as to who would make the first sighting, on which day, at what time and where. Everyone was excited, and individuals frequently got to their feet to scan the horizon for the long-promised land.

Conversation became general. Everyone had something to say about what he would do on getting ashore. There was talk about favourite meals, restaurants where the austerity of the U.K. would not apply. One man announced that the first thing he was going to do was drink six pints of ale – while studying the menu! Most of us, however, were prepared to settle for plain fish-and-chips. The chief officer promised a bottle of champagne to the first man to make a sighting and there was much laughter and joking. But the euphoria could not for long resist the discomfort and inevitable doubts. By nightfall the boat was virtually silent.

Squally weather came on again with nightfall, frequent refreshing showers which, however, kept us awake, wet and uncomfortable. The water collected, mainly from areas of canvas, was brackish still, but we had got used to the taste by now and it was a very welcome supplement to our regular rations. With our sails full of wind and straining the boat pressed forward, the sound of water rushing along the hull a delight and entertainment – such a contrast to doldrum days of intolerable heat.

Early dawn on day eleven. I was sitting in my favourite position, up front, my leg dangling over the side. The squalls had passed; we moved slowly through a rippling sea, glossy, almost flat calm, a-gleam under the lightening sky. A bright point on the horizon marked where the sun's ball of red fire was about to emerge. Half dozing, I glanced down at my leg – and saw and immediately scooped up a twig with three green leaves. A great surge of delight and relief passed through me – like the dove sent from the Ark, I had found the first sign of dry land. I scrambled to my feet and scanned the horizon minutely, straining on tiptoes to increase my height to the maximum. Nothing. No further sign, either, of twigs or leaves. But my excitement was not diminished and I shouted my shipmates awake, waving my leafy twig and pointing ahead.

There was intense discussion as to how there could be twigs and leaves floating, but no sight of land. Evidently land could not be far distant. The twig must have been washed down some large river into the prevailing southeasterly current off the Bulge of Africa. Optimism and excitement brought demands for increased rations, but the senior officers rejected this out of hand: we might yet be many days' sailing from land. What's more, there was still the danger of being swept southerly into the Bight of Benin.

The next two days and nights dragged by, cruelly tormenting. The wind dropped. There was only one squall, and that a light one. All day, the sea surged flat and glossy, though there were intermittent patches of twigs and leaves. Had we drifted too far south? During the flat calms we made efforts to row, but only exhausted ourselves into fits of gasping and coughing, and to no visible effect. The sun's heat had grown more intense and most of us suffered, for the first time, from painful sunburn – presumably this was an effect of the proximity of land. Wind was our only salvation, and we knew it, and every one of us silently prayed for it.

Day fourteen. Still no sight of land. The sea glossy, flat calm. I was seated in my usual position in the bow. Standing, for any length of time, had become impossible. We were making no headway that I could detect, drifting sideways, I thought, on the current, with a scattering of twigs and leaves. Every so often I screwed my eyes up and stared ahead, willing land to emerge, but there was nothing to be seen except a low misty haze across the entire horizon. It was disappointing, but I had not seen the phenomenon before, and it interested me.

I dozed in the early-morning warmth, wondering idly what the significance of this haze was, wishing it to be land, but unable to see any break or indication. Be patient, I told myself, hold on. We drifted in silence.

About half an hour later I opened my eyes to see the full sun clear above the horizon. The haze was gone. In its place I saw . . . a dark stretch? A scattering of short, vertical lines? Land? Coconut palms? I opened my mouth to shout, 'Land ahead!' And shut it again. A mirage? If I did shout, and got it wrong, I'd be lynched. 'Wait, Jones,' I told myself. 'Control yourself. There's no hurry.' I hauled myself

48

painfully to my feet, bracing myself against the mast and scanned the horizon with minute attention. Under the strengthening sun the view became clearer every moment. There was no further doubt: ahead was a flat, low-lying coast with scattered palm trees. 'Land ahead!' I yelled. 'Land ahead!' my voice shattering the dawn silence. Within seconds the wakened crew were causing the boat to list by hanging over the leeboard side to get a clear view of the coastline. Great joy was felt by everyone – but the three Asian stokers in the bow made no attempt to emerge from the security of their locker home.

The one-spirit floating compass that led us safely to land.

Chapter Four

Land ahead – but what land was it? There were several possibilities, not all of them good: Senegal (not good – Vichy France), Sierre Leone (best of all – British), Liberia (good enough – allied to the United States). Exhaustion was forgotten, fourteen days of hell put behind us, as the adrenalin began to flow.

Landfall, however, is one thing; landing quite another. After a babble of conflicting suggestions, we realised that the boat was again becalmed and it could well be nightfall before we reached shore – five or six miles distant still, by our reckoning. Double rations were issued and serious discussion began. What if this *was* Senegal? How were we to confront our enemies? The very idea of confrontation was laughable: our gross armament comprised the oars, two blunt, rusty boat-axes and a couple of small knives – and the combination of weakness and the long period of inaction meant that if we were able to stand up, on landing, that would be the most we could manage.

Landing was, in any case, not going to be straightforward. There was a moderate swell running, directly onto a steeply shelving foreshore with hidden reefs of coral. How were we to keep our boat's head to shore as we ran in through the heavy, breaking rollers? We decided that if we could not make the beach by dusk we would have to use the canvas sea-anchor and ride the night out a mile offshore – getting safely ashore was going to be difficult enough by daylight. What if the boat turned beam on to the rollers? We could be swamped, thrown into the surf and, in our weakened condition, lose our lives on the very verge of safety. But the need to be ashore overpowered rational considerations and, with all the time in the world to come to safe, practical conclusions, the consensus was to hold steady for shore and the speediest landing.

A second round of double rations was served at midday and, strengthened by these, we reviewed our plan of campaign. Suppose that it was Liberia we had reached, should we, having ascertained our position, replenish our water supplies, obtain food from friendly natives and sail on? Absurd! We had not strength enough to row, let alone free the lifeboat from soft sand and launch it against those rollers. We might hold offshore on the sea-anchor and send a party ashore to scout the immediate area. Several hotheads volunteered for this, but it was equally absurd; none of us was strong enough to fight the undercurrents, and even if anyone did manage to get safely ashore, he could never get back.

Our increasingly excited discussions were rudely interrupted by the lookout reporting black dots or shapes heading out towards us. It was about 2 p.m. by now, and soon the shapes revealed themselves as three or four large canoes with tiny sails. As they came closer we were able to see native fishermen paddling steadily. Consternation! Were we about to come under attack? We agreed to defend ourselves against boarders with the oars – far too heavy to manhandle – axes and knives. The canoes were soon close enough for us to make out the fine physique of their occupants: tall, slim, well-muscled, ebony-black Africans with pearly white teeth.

There were six canoes in all and the first, manned by four natives, reversed paddles and stopped about thirty feet away. Were they waiting for reinforcements before the attack? There were enough of them to surround us. We would have no chance at all.

The men waved and smiled, but remained silent, staring at us. Then they seemed to sense our anxiety, for a man stood up in the stern of one canoe and shouted, 'We Christians!' Blessed relief! Magic to our ears – they were friendly. 'What country?' we called back. 'Liberia,' he said, and we cheered and clapped and beckoned them alongside.

Soon there was a group of four canoes around us, each twenty-five to thirty feet long, hand cut and with practically no freeboard. Their occupants stared at us with friendly, smiling faces while large fish floated about their feet. This, we learned later, was the village co-operative fishing fleet. We managed, with pidgin-English, to communicate with two of our rescuers while the remainder, unable to converse, looked on with broad smiles. We asked about fresh water and food. 'Yea,' they said – we would soon learn that 'We Christians' and 'Yea' comprised the bulk of their English vocabulary. They understood more English than they spoke, however, and reacted to our conversation by nodding or shaking their heads. We would not allow any of them on board at first, unsure whether we could trust them. Should we beach now, or anchor off and attempt to have supplies brought out?

After brief discussion we concluded that the natives were friendly and that we could not face any further voyaging. With a combination of pidgin and mime – putting the rowlocks into their slots, pointing to the oars and miming the act of rowing – we managed to convey a request for help. Five smiling fisherman, naked except for coloured print loin-cloths, now came on board, nearly capsizing their canoes as they did so. We lowered our sails and sat back to watch the efforts of our new crew.

Meanwhile the remaining canoes took the vacated ones in tow and went ahead to inform their village of our impending arrival. We soon discovered that our new oarsmen were not going to get their Blues: they were not accustomed to oars, got insufficient dip on them, and kept catching crabs. By sitting alongside them, our hands close to theirs on the oars, we helped them master the technique of rowing a wide-beam, flat-bottomed lifeboat. Soon, slowly but steadily, the shore line closed and we were able to make out miles and miles of golden sand stretching away as far as eye could see.

The beach was about four hundred feet wide, then there was a green-brown ridge, soil with some grass, apparently, which merged into high shrubby undergrowth, banana trees and coconut palms. The village was out of sight, its position marked by smoke rising above dense undergrowth – a homing beacon for men fishing three or four miles offshore.

After two hours' rowing, with regular breaks for rest, we still had not reached shore. Our apprehensions were dying away and our anticipation sharpening, but we reckoned it would take a further two hours before we were on dry land. Our new friends must have been puzzled to find such a motley crew on their fishing grounds, but I think they realised that we were survivors from a shipwreck. Their colleagues seemed already to have spread the word because people were emerging from the undergrowth and forming a welcoming party on the shore.

Gradually we edged closer, until the spray from white, foaming breakers made a haze beweeen us and the shore. The fishermen, accustomed to the skill by now, rowed steadily on, pointing to their people gathered on the shore and indicating that we should steer towards them. I was in my favourite position up in the bow, both legs dangling in the water and my eyes fixed on the reception party. Just before we entered the zone of white-topped breakers one of the fishermen took the tiller and the bow immediately swung round. We were not safe yet.

Once into the rollers there was no turning back. We were on a roller-coaster ride, yawing wildly at times, but kept, by our friends' skill or good fortune, more or less on course. It was odd to see the shore party appear sometimes on the port bow and the next moment to starboard. A dozen or so natives had waded waist-high into the sea, waving a welcome, and those on shore waved also and danced in their excitement. In the midst of all this a voice from the stern shouted, 'Jones! Put this on and land with dignity.' Someone had discovered in his emergency bag one scarf, R.A.F. blue, hand-knitted, H.M. Forces for the comfort of, supplied, no doubt, by some kindly Women's Institute or church group. Six feet or so long, it went twice around my then slim waist and formed a loin-cloth sufficient to avoid a full frontal encounter with our prospective hosts.

I have, to this day, no idea who it was who produced, so late in the day, this covering for my nakedness. Had it been made available at the beginning of our voyage it would have been very acceptable indeed, a shield for my back and shoulders against the fierce sun and a protection at night for my injured foot which was constantly being knocked or trodden on. Had my comrade been loath to part with something that might come in handy for himself? Such is human nature. I was very thankful, nevertheless, for small mercies – clothed again, after all this time, however inadequately.

The boat was rolling and yawing wildly now and we clung on tightly, afraid we might capsize in the heavy, breaking rollers. It was clear that few, if any, of us would survive the undercurrents if this were to happen. Then, suddenly, it was all over: a dozen men at least seized the grablines and ran us in to the full limit of our flotation. We dragged to a halt at an angle of twenty-five degrees, in two feet of foamy water.

Home from sea. Liberia, West Africa. 17.20 hours. Latitude 4° 58' North, Longitude 9° West, close to Nour Point. More than 1,200 miles from where we had been sunk. A considerable achievement and one which was to bring our senior officer a richly deserved O.B.E.

From my position I was the first to set foot on shore. Foolishly, without pausing for thought, I jumped into the water and fell flat on my face as my weakened legs gave way under me. Two smiling villagers seized my arms and carried me up to the soft, dry sand where I was immediately surrounded by friendly faces. Impossible to describe my happiness and relief – it was a kind of resurrection. But I was very concerned at my inability to stand without overbalancing, let alone walk. The beach rose and fell beneath my feet with the habitual motion of fourteen days afloat.

Last off were our three Asians. They had clung to their home in the bow-locker until the last and had to be carried, bent almost double by their long, cramped confinement, and their legs and backs massaged before they could move at all freely. Two thirds at least of my shipmates suffered the same problems of balance as I did and none of us was able to walk normally for more than twenty-four hours.

We gathered in a circle with our hosts to plan our future. They handed us fresh bananas, our first solid food for a fortnight, half-coconuts full of exquisitely refreshing 'milk' and gallon cans of fresh water, champagne to our lips, which we passed from man to man until our long thirst was slaked. Two villagers had a reasonable command of English and, when we asked how far we were from the nearest town, replied, 'Marshall Field' (an American base 120 miles up the coast). We had landed approximately 180 miles south-east of Liberia's capital, Monrovia.

Of course there could be no question of our walking twelve, let alone 120 miles in oppressive heat along that shore in our weak and rundown condition, but we left it an open option for when we had regained strength. This troubled me, for I had severe doubts whether I should be able to cope: my injury compelled me to walk on the ball of the foot to avoid pressure on the torn and open ankle.

The two spokesmen took our senior officers away to meet their chief and discuss arrangements for housing and feeding us. The rest of us now had time to study our new friends who had gathered in a circle around us, looking, smiling and chattering in their own language. The men wore a kind of skirt of printed cotton which reached as far as their knees. The women's skirts were longer, reaching to their ankles, and their breasts were bare. Around their necks they wore strings of beads and cowrie shells. Many of them had blue tattoos on arms and chest. The older girls wore around their waists a short cotton cloth with bead decoration and children up to the age of eight or so went naked. These children were to become our best friends and would follow us about all day and every day; we used to play football with them and help them sail their hand-carved model canoes on the pond.

The young men of the village were now investigating our boat, so

Michael and I went aboard to find souvenirs. I salvaged the compass, and Michael the cork plug bungs – items which would be a talking-point between us for the next fifty-four years. I always maintained that without the compass we should never have made land; Michael would retort, 'Without the bungs the boat would have been waterlogged.'

The young men now decided to move the lifeboat and insisted on doing so in spite of our appeals to them to leave it in the shallow water to prevent the seams springing in the heat. Within minutes they had managed to overturn that twenty-five-foot, heavy lifeboat, and there, before our eyes, was our last home turned turtle on a hostile shore. There was little hope now of continuing our voyage along the coast – without help from the villagers we should never be able to right it. Our survival was firmly in the Liberians' hands unless we could somehow get a message to Marshall Field or Monrovia.

The senior officers returned just before sunset. It had been agreed that we should sleep on the soft sand that night and that the Chief would arrange for us to be billeted next day with families who had spare accommodation in their mud huts or in huts used for storage. It had been further agreed that the British Government should reimburse the costs of our food and accommodation – though to this day I have no idea of the sum agreed or how – or, indeed, if – a final payment was ever made.

Agitation broke out among the villagers surrounding the lifeboat. They could not agree on how best to convey it to the village. We begged them to leave it where it was, but they ignored us. Eventually it was carried, upside down, to the edge of the undergrowth, turned over onto its keel and then, by means of rollers, pushed down the well-worn path to the village. There it was ceremonially deposited, upside down, in front of the Chief's hut. For the time being this was the resting place of the unglamorous vessel which had saved the lives of twenty-one men and for which each of them had considerable affection, in spite of its discomforts. I wonder what became of it? It was too heavy for fishing – launching and recovery would have been extremely difficult. Probably it was bartered inland for goats, perhaps to be used as a ferry on the River Sangwin.

It had been a long, exciting day, but nobody was ready for sleep. As the sun began to set the villagers made for home, leaving us alone on the clean, soft, golden sand to receive information and advice from

55

our officers. Village life, they said, worked as a kind of co-operative, with the men fishing and the women cooking, doing the chores and cultivating small allotments where maize, sweet potatoes and other vegetables were grown. It was the women's job also to carry on their heads the cans filled with fresh water from a deep spring about a quarter of a mile away. The Chief had issued a number of directives: we must conduct ourselves according to his law and pay him due respect when seated outside his hut. We were also to treat the women with respect and there was to be no fraternisation. We must not pick bananas, coconuts or any other fruit without his permission. All that was required, however, was to ask the children to approach him with our request to do so.

We slept in a circle, feet inward, unsure what dangers there might be from wildlife. We knew there were snakes and later learned of large cats and other predators. As I lay there, the beauty of the star-filled sky overhead, I had very mixed feelings. It was wonderful to be safe from drowning or death by thirst or starvation, but a torment to be unable to let my mother and family know that I was safe. And I was worried about my open wound: how long would I be able to keep it free of serious infection now that I would have to walk over sand and soil to bathe it in sea water? Would I get proper medical attention in time?

It was an uncomfortable night physically for all of us. We had gorged ourselves with food and drunk large quantities of water, and now our stomachs protested with loud and frequent rumblings. My belly was painfully distended and I left the circle several times in the hope of achieving my first bowel-movement for two weeks. Daybreak arrived without my having managed it, but this did not prevent my looking eagerly forward to a cooked meal.

Daybreak brought intensive activity to the beach. The fishermen, assisted by their wives and children, were preparing their canoes for the long day's fishing. As soon as the canoes were ready they were assisted out into the rollers, the men paddling furiously to make their way over the white crests. Once clear of danger, they waved their paddles to indicate that all was well. Then they pulled steadily away to make up for time lost the previous day.

We were looking forward to our first sight of the village and a meeting with the Chief. We bathed in the sea and queued for the comb to make ourselves as presentable as we could. Most of us had untidy beards and altogether we looked, in spite of our best efforts, bedraggled, haggard and worn out. At about 8 a.m. the Chief's eldest son arrived to escort us to our audience with his father. He explained that the latter would not be able to converse with us and that we should show our respect for his position by shaking his hand.

Our excitement was almost as intense as it had been on sighting land the previous day. We walked two or three abreast, some of the children friendly enough to hold our hands as they chattered away to one another, happy to have found new friends in these complete and unexpected strangers. We found out later that they had never seen a white man before and that this was why many of them were unwilling or afraid at first to take our proffered hands. It was to be some days before we were fully accepted by young and old alike.

On leaving the foreshore we found ourselves on sand-based green turf, soft and moist to the feet. Swaying palm trees towered over us, their coconuts bunched near the top. Even if we got permission, there was no way we were going to climb the sixty feet to pick them. We continued along a well-worn path of beaten earth, the undergrowth closing in around us, darkening the whole area and cutting off the direct rays of sunlight so that it was pleasantly cool. After about a quarter of a mile we began to see small sunlit clearings to left and right. These were the allotments in which vegetables were grown. All the banana trees, coconut palms and oil palms were the sole property of the Chief.

Now we saw paths converging ahead into the large clearing which contained the village. Its well-trodden earth floor was swept clean and as we arrived families came out of their huts smiling and joined our procession. There was already a large welcoming crowd gathered in front of the Chief's hut.

He was a man of seventy or so, but heat and humidity had wizened him into the appearance of one ten years older. He was a congenial person, with a ready smile, proud of his title and the respect it brought him from his subjects. He had two wives and eight children and owed his position not to hereditary right but to political appointment from Monrovia, whence supervision was exercised quarterly by a government official carried in a sedan chair by four bearers. He sat outside his hut on a bamboo throne with a tall, fanned back and wide armrests and wore a white, calf-length cotton robe which left one shoulder bare. On the right of the chair were displayed his credentials, a parchment eighteen inches by twelve, framed behind glass. This bore a government stamp and the signature of President Tubman and identified him as Chief of this area.

He wore a necklace of what I took to be ivory but proved on closer inspection to be bone in alternating strips of white and brown. Pinned to the right side of his robe at chest level was an oval enamelled brooch similar in colour to the framed parchment at his feet – his badge of office, worn only on official occasions and when the government official made his quarterly visit. The Chief was surrounded by his wives, his children and his grandchildren, all of them smiling broadly at us as we approached. We paid our respects by shaking the proffered hand. When I stepped forward I could see him casting a curious look at my unusual loin-cloth, but his main interest was in the compass which I was carrying in my left hand. I handed it to him and he took it in both hands and was intrigued by the card revolving in its flotation. He was amused by our various possessions: the two axes with daily notches on their handles, cork bung plugs attached to brass chain, the galvanised dippers for measuring out the water-ration, wooden handled balers, two cans of Omnipon tablets and torn blankets stiff with salt. It required no translator to explain how badly we needed his hospitality.

When the ceremony of welcome was concluded, we were asked to form a line so that those villagers with room to accommodate us could make their selection – it was rather as if the slave-trade, in reverse, had returned to Africa. I placed myself next to Michael, who, with his blonde hair and beard was a centre of attraction, hoping that we might find ourselves billeted together. When he was chosen, I stepped forward with him – we were holding hands, in fact – but I was rejected and he shared a hut with a sailor and the radio officer. I was chosen together with two able-bodied seamen and, after some confusing discussion, it emerged that we were to share a hut about half a mile away. I asked the senior officer to point out my difficulty in walking so far, and he did so, but it made no difference.

We were all keen to see our accommodation, but what about breakfast and lunch? There was plenty of fresh water, fruit and coconuts, but no sign as yet of the cooked meal we were all longing for. Before we dispersed, however, we were told to gather outside the Chief's hut at sunset for an evening meal and entertainment.

We dispersed to our new homes, all in the village except for that of myself and my two shipmates. The three of us were taken, by our host, his family and a motley band of adults and children, along the bush-path which ran parallel to the foreshore. After the close, cramped community of the boat I felt a sudden sense of loneliness. With the excitement of the previous day over, there was a feeling of reaction, a paradoxical disappointment. How were we to move on from here? Re-launching the lifeboat – which was apparently being held in part-payment for our board and lodging – was virtually out of the question (and soon became completely so when the villagers ignored our request to fill it with water to prevent shrinkage and, within forty-eight hours, most of the seams opened).

The path was soft and the stirred-up dust irritated my open wound, but eventually we reached what I can only describe as the equivalent of a Welsh hamlet 'out in the sticks'. About twenty minutes away from the Chief's seat of government, it was much smaller and had only about half as many inhabitants. They had all turned out to greet us, though, their broad smiles showing the beautiful white teeth which were possessed by young and old alike. We soon learned the secret of these – people would sit for hours around their open fires and, as they did so, work away at their teeth with soft wooden brushes rather like the woody liquorice sticks that were popular when I was a schoolboy. In such a primitive community survival to any great age would depend on good teeth.

There were two types of hut. The larger was of square design with a sloped roof that extended well beyond the walls so as to shed rainwater clear of them. Both roof and walls were of latticed split bamboo, the former waterproofed with a coating of clay, inside and out. In order to allow free circulation of air, the walls had no such coating. The one large room was home for a whole family. Our home was in a smaller adjacent hut, circular in shape. Its furnishings comprised one split bamboo mattress, six feet by three and supported six inches clear of the bare, earthen floor, to sleep three persons.

When the men were not out fishing they liked to take their beds out of the huts and lounge on them in the shade, endlessly talking, perhaps about the big one that got away. We never saw the women lounge about like this: they worked hard all day, tending their crops, carrying water and grinding the maize which was an important part of their diet. This process was fascinating: the cobs were put into a hollowed-out log about three feet high and two or three women, working together, would pummel them with heavy wooden crushers, six feet long. The work was hard and their timing and rhythm – each crusher striking in succession, somewhat like a peal of bells – extraordinary. They appeared to be happy at their work, for they chatted non-stop. Children were always kept close by, within their mothers' sight and although no man would so far compromise his dignity as to engage in domestic chores, fathers often took care of them.

As soon as we were settled in our hut I asked our host, in the best sign language I could muster, if I could have a wash in fresh water. He understood almost at once, bless him, and directed his wife to fetch some. When she returned she led me by the hand to the back of their hut where their bathroom was set up behind six-foot bamboo fences. She indicated that I should go inside, then handed me – a thick bar of Sunlight Carbolic, the first soap of any kind that I had seen since my shower had been so rudely interrupted fifteen days before. Their shower was unique – a one gallon water can pierced with numerous nail-holes. What about the water, I was wondering, when the lady of the house appeared above my head and began pouring it into the pierced can. This first shower with soap was heavenly: the pierced holes were so small that a gallon of water seemed to last for ever. After the luxury of the shower I looked around for a towel, but in this climate such accessories were neither used nor necessary. I was dry within minutes without one.

Fully dressed again (in my scarf) I returned to thank my host. He was sitting out on his bed, and indicated that I should join him, then pointed to my foot and called his wife over to examine what was now a very ugly-looking gash. She called in several other women for a consultation, and they examined the foot with great care, gently prodding and squeezing it to open the wound. There was a gasp as they saw the bared bone. After a little more discussion they fetched warm boiled water, bathed the wound and bandaged it with a strip of old, but clean cloth. At last there was some degree of comfort, and I was extremely grateful.

An hour before sunset we set off for the Chief's feast. On rejoining our comrades, we were conspicuous for our unruly hair – the comb had been retained at the village. A huge log fire burned in the square and the entire population had gathered to welcome us. The Chief was served first, then the rest of us received our portions in a collection of chipped enamelled plates and cups. There was no cutlery: everyone ate with their fingers. First came a hot pepper soup, then sweet potato and fish cooked in palm-oil. I enjoyed the potato, but in the darkness could not make out what portion of the fish's anatomy I had received. Nor did my best efforts yield anything edible. Although the food was unfamiliar and not very satisfying, it did mark a significant stage in our return to civilization.

When the eating was over we decided to contribute to the entertainment with a rendering of 'John Brown's Body'. To our great surprise, the children joined in: it seems that a Roman Catholic missionary visited the village regularly and had taught them to sing hymns in their native tongue. It was a deeply emotional experience to hear those pure young voices there in the Liberian bush, so far from our own loved ones. Then they sang, in pidgin-English, what must have been a tribute to our position: 'O, Mama, when shall we see our home, when shall we see our Mama and Papa, when shall we see our home?' and there was not one of us who did not have tears in his eyes.

The night, too, was beautiful, the tropical moon almost as bright as day, but as we returned to our hut I was feeling uncomfortable again, my belly distended and rumbling. We sat up for a while around our own village fire, reminiscing about a voyage that was already beginning to seem unreal. Then we settled our positions under the communal lifeboat blanket on the communal bamboo bed. Being the youngest and smallest, I had the middle place – and it was something of an experience, dressed in nothing but my borrowed scarf, to bed down between the two strapping able seamen. We all saw the funny side, though, and in any case were so exhausted that we fell deeply asleep almost immediately.

I was awakened early next morning by something falling on my face. I sat up in the darkness and found fragments of mud from the roof. I could hear rain falling outside, but this mud was dry, so it was not rain that had brought it down. Later I learned that large spiders were active in the roof at night and that they were responsible.

My two shipmates were snoring loudly on either side of me, so I tried to get back to sleep, but was prevented by the discomfort in my belly. This rapidly became worse, so I made a careful dash for the door. Outside, in the torrential rain, you could not see your hand in front of your face, but I moved as rapidly as I dared in what I hoped was the direction of the beach. The bush at night is a strange, eerie place. Frogs, in particular, send out their mating calls from sunset to sunrise. With a bit of luck I gained the soft sand, squatted down and, almost literally, exploded. Never, before or since, have I experienced such glorious relief from prolonged constipation. I returned, exhausted and soaked, to the hamlet and spent the remainder of the night alternately sitting by the remains of the fire, clasping a very uncomfortable abdomen, and making further hurried visits to the foreshore.

The village came back to bustling life with the dawn. It was still not fully day when we were handed our breakfast – two large fish-heads and a tail on a bed of rice. We buried it in the soft sand of the shore, hoping for something better next time and returned to observe the daily routine of village life.

In each hut the fire would be lit before sunrise, water boiled and then breakfast cooked. Boys were responsible for collecting wood; girls helped their mothers prepare the meal and wash the cooking utensils; adult males lounged about, discussing their plans for the day's fishing. As soon as their tasks were done, the children were free to play.

They were particularly fond of football, and many of the younger sailors joined them in kicking the small, soft ball about. Playing along the paths, especially running with hoops was popular, but they also made models of their fathers' canoes and sailed them on the village ponds. All of them were adept in the use of a knife for hunting, fishing and carving: they made me a model canoe, perfect in shape and contours, and smoothed with a piece of broken glass and by rubbing with sand. They would also scour the shore for the sand-crabs which the men used for bait.

The community did, indeed, function as a co-operative. Fish was both their main food and a product to be bartered with neighbouring villages for chickens and goats which were allowed to roam freely about the village under communal ownership. Land transport comprised four or five ancient Raleigh bicycles with solid tyres. These were used to transport the fish, which was hung over the handlebars and along the crossbars. At first I had hoped that we might have at least one egg a day, perhaps fried in palm-oil, or some goats' milk – even, occasionally, roasted goat. But the daily fare never varied: fish heads and tails morning and evening and never a chip to go with them.

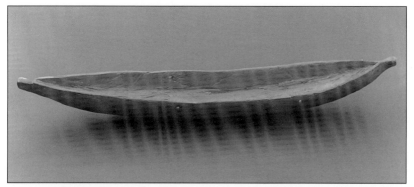
Model fishing canoe – made by the children and presented as a gift.

On our first morning we received word to proceed to the Chief's village as soon as breakfast was over. All twenty-one of us assembled to discuss our present position and future actions. The first subject to come up was the fish heads and tails, and the senior officer said that he had already planned a meeting with the Chief to talk about this. We discussed ways and means of sending a message up the coast or through the bush, perhaps with the help of travellers who went bartering from village to village. We decided to try and recruit a young fisherman to carry a letter up the coast, accompanied by a volunteer survivor, but this came to nothing: we had four volunteers, but no young fisherman and no canoe. It was agreed that all travellers who passed through would be asked to report our arrival, in the hope that word would eventually spread to Monrovia or 'Robert Field'.

When the latter was mentioned I reported that, during my shuttling back and forth in the night, I thought I had heard aircraft engines at high altitude, but no one else had heard anything and the general view was that I had imagined it. At my suggestion, the village interpreter was asked whether they ever saw aircraft passing over and he said that the fishermen had seen single aircraft passing over about two miles from shore. We enquired about their course and he pointed north, then swung his arm round 180°; we hopefully assumed that this meant the aircraft were on the regular R.A.F. patrol out of Freetown on sweep-searches for enemy submarines and survivors.

We discussed measures to attract the attention of any aircraft which might pass and a large bonfire on the foreshore was suggested. I pointed out, however, that pilots would be accustomed to smoke rising from the bush and assume it was from the villages. What, then, might be employed instead? We decided to construct a large S O S in the sand and when we put this suggestion to the Chief he told the children to help us.

We began by scooping out the letters with paddles from the canoes while the children, perhaps thinking that we were building them sandcastles, ran around and all over them. When we had finished, and stepped away to admire our work, we had to agree that it was quite useless: we could hardly make it out ourselves. After further consideration we decided that we should never manage a visible marker in the soft, yellow sand and tried the hard, wet sand instead. This produced a more distinct S O S, but we were still not happy and adjourned for further thought during the night.

Back at the village, we reported our progress to the Chief and said that we would make a further effort next morning. The Chief, who had noticed that I was walking with a limp, pointed to my bandaged foot and inquired whether I was in pain. I was, indeed, suffering pain, up near the thigh, and indicated this, whereupon he asked to see the wound and called his wives and other women to inspect it. They recommended that I should allow them to apply their medicine and produced a greyish mud-pack with leaves protruding from it. I refused because although it was clear that infection had spread up my leg, I feared that the village medicine might cause gangrene. The villagers themselves, however, seemed to enjoy excellent health and to know how to treat sickness and injuries. There were no trained midwives or doctors, but many happy, healthy children, a credit to their mothers. Nevertheless, I preferred my pain to their uncertain remedy.

In our poor physical state the labour on the shore had exhausted us and the half-mile walk back home was hard to manage. After sunset the evening meal appeared, as unappetizing as ever, though one of my companions had managed to develop a taste for fish-eyes,which he swallowed whole like oysters. The night was fine and clear and my gastric trouble, assisted by abstention from fruit, was clearing up. My appetite, as a result, was sharpening and I had begun to long for a decent hot meal. When we went to bed we were very pleased to find that our filthy, salt-soaked blanket had been thoroughly washed and was soft again. This helped me enjoy my first really good night's sleep since the sinking, quite oblivious to the fact that the gastric upsets had reached both of my bedfellows and had them up and down all night.

After breakfast we set off again for the main village, discussing our S O S project. To save my wound from the dusty path, I left my companions and walked along the foreshore, over the clean golden sand. My attention was caught by the lush green palm leaves, each of them up to ten feet long, swaying in the breeze. When we were discussing our next step I suggested that we might construct our signal from these, but the Chief Officer said that he had already considered it and was reluctant to strip the trees of their leaves. He consulted the Chief, however, who consented to the use of two leaves per tree – any more might cause serious damage to the palm and its fruit, which, deprived of shade, would dry up under direct sunlight. The children were again told to help, and set off, armed with machetes, for another happy day on the beach with the white people.

The teenagers swiftly climbed the forty-foot trees and sent two leaves from each crashing to the ground, along with a few coconuts whose milk we drank when thirsty. The younger children helped us drag the leaves down to the shore, and soon we had a small mountain of them. The green of the leaves stood out well against the gold of the sand, so we decided to place them in the soft rather than the hard sand. Again our design team outlined S O S in the sand, and the children, who had begun to understand what was required, rushed to help fill the letter-shapes with green. By mid afternoon we had completed the design – but we were not happy with it. It was necessary to lengthen each letter and make the gaps between them wider. By early evening we had completed the signal to our satisfaction. All that was required now was a low-flying aircraft.

As we returned along the shore, two of the sailors decided to cool off in the sea, so I took the opportunity to bathe my foot in salt water again. The children accompanied us – the older ones were accomplished swimmers, but the young ones were content to paddle with me at the edge. Two days had forged a close friendship between us and the children: they were proud and happy now to hold our hands and we could not go anywhere without their company.

That evening brought heavy showers which developed into a tropical downpour that lasted all night. The huts were to some extent protected from direct rainfall by overhanging trees, but within an hour the dry clearing had been transformed into a lake. Many huts, ours included, were flooded so that we had to spend the night sitting on our bed, reminiscing and wondering what tomorrow would bring.

As soon as the sun rose, steam billowed up everywhere, bringing a strong smell of leafy undergrowth mixed with smoke and spices. From the kitchen came the less attractive smell of fish-heads frying in oil over an open wood fire. At breakfast we were given our first hot drink, coffee, apparently, from local beans, very acceptable to the palate. Like Oliver Twist, we asked for more; unlike Oliver were were readily given some.

We set off cheerfully for our morning rendezvous, the children running on ahead or clinging to our hands. The sun was a ball of fire and the bush a turkish bath, so we walked along the cooler foreshore. A crowd had gathered at the point where our S O S had been created and we soon realised why. It was in tatters, disarranged, unrecognizable, unreadable alike from land or air. During the night the goats, carefully penned up each dusk for safety, had been visited by a leopard which had smashed down their door and made off with one of their number. The rest, having dispersed in panic to the foreshore, had found compensation in the appetising meal laid out there and had eaten most of it.

After the goats had been rounded up and returned to the village, it was agreed that the children would shepherd them during daylight hours and keep them away from our signal. We started again from scratch, but, improved by practice, not only made a better S O S, but added our vessel's international registered call-sign, G M P R. We stood back and admired the bright green lettering conspicuous against its sandy background. But we had doubts as to whether patrolling aircraft would deviate far enough from their regular route to pick it out. Every night now we heard heavy aircraft passing at high altitude – on course, we learned later, from the U.S.A. to R.A.F. Egypt via the Ascension Islands and Roberts Field, Liberia.

We resolved to add a string to our bow by sending a group of six volunteers from among the fittest men, accompanied by two villagers as guides, to trek through the bush to Roberts Field and report our survival, hoping then to be rescued by helicopter or from the sea. Someone spotted an aircraft seaward to the north, on a course parallel to the coastline, and we all became extremely excited, waving whatever came to hand while the children danced with joy and ran towards the sea, waving their arms. We timed it from first appearance at 12.40 p.m. to its disappearance to the south-west, four or five minutes later, and estimated its altitude at eight to ten thousand feet.

There was no sign of recognition: the aircraft maintained its course steadily and soon the noise of its engines died away, leaving us frustrated and downcast. However, we now set up a daily vigil of four-hour watches so that there would always be someone present in daylight to try and catch attention. I was excused this because of the long walk, but volunteered to take part every second day.

As the days dragged on, it became clear that patrolling aircraft did not pass regularly, even at a distance. Perhaps U-boat activity had intensified and patrols were being re-organised to cope with this. We kept watch and, while we were waiting, learned more about the life and customs of our temporary home.

Liberia had a fairly scattered population of some three million people. In the north there was considerable economic development, with vast rubber plantations supplying raw materials to the United States car industry. President Tubman had been educated in the U.S.A. and was naturally on their side against the Axis powers, very willing to allow the use of the port facilities at Marshall and the air base at Roberts. The south-east, where we had landed, was economically far less developed and comprised dense forest and bush from the coast to the border with the Ivory Coast, the whole area rich in such wild-life as tropical birds, monkeys, baboons and leopards. The main activity was subsistence agriculture, with fishing on the coast; the main trading activity, barter.

When the men from our village were at sea a constant lookout was kept so that as soon as they were seen returning the rest of the villagers could assemble to help them land and sort the catch. This would be laid out on the beach, the portion for local consumption determined by two elders and shared out there and then among the families. The women would carry their portion away in enamel pans balanced on their heads and make their way back home to prepare the evening meal. The teenagers would carry the rest to the village, where it would be gutted in readiness for sale or barter early the following morning. The fishermen, meanwhile, remained with their canoes to wash them out and prepare lines and hooks for the following day's fishing.

A substantial catch meant a day or two of holiday for the fishermen and they spent the time lounging and chatting on the foreshore under the cool of the palm trees. To reduce the hard labour of paddling out to the fishing-grounds, each large canoe had a mast and small sail.

The building of a canoe, a highly skilled occupation, was carried on in a designated area under the trees known to us as The Shipyard. Up to six 'shipwrights' worked there, assisted by six young 'apprentices' learning the craft from their fathers.

The process was long and complicated and began with the selection of a suitable forty-foot tree. The search for this could occupy several days, and when it was found the Chief's permission had to be obtained to fell it. Two elders would inspect it on his behalf and report back. All the able-bodied men of the village would then be recruited to transport the trunk back, often from deep in the forest, by means of rollers along one of the bush-paths to 'the shipyard'.

The trunk would then be supported and securely wedged at a convenient height and the shipwrights would set to work with their short-handled adzes. The craftsmanship was extraordinary: without plans or drawing a perfectly balanced dug-out was produced, its bow and stern of similar design. The outer surface of the hull was planed down with pieces of broken glass, a process which took many hours of laborious work. Then a smooth finish was achieved by repeated rubbing in the soft sand of the foreshore. The glass came from oil bottles obtained from the sale or barter of fish.

The launch of a new canoe was an important ceremonial occasion attended by the entire village. Everyone lent a hand to carry it down to the sea and assist it through the breakers. When it was clear, the sail would be hoisted to the accompaniment of loud cheering from the shore. It was not clear to us whether the canoes were regarded as the property of the Chief or the co-operative, but each one had its own crew responsible for sailing and maintaining it. Today, fifty-four years later, canoes are still constructed by hand, but now they are made with a square stern to take an outboard motor and cover great distances both to fish and on their trips up and down the coast to sell their catch.

In spite of primitive living conditions, lack of sanitation, flies and malaria-carrying mosquitos, the villagers' health seemed extremely good. This was fortunate, for they had no health service, no G.P. and the nearest hospital was in Monrovia. They were all very clean in appearance, with shining, smooth ebony skin and extraordinarily white teeth. The young males were of splendid physique: tall, slim, without an ounce of surplus fat, they would have had a good chance in any Mr World Contest. The women were tall, with high cheekbones and intricately plaited hair. Younger women wore nothing above the

All the children seemed perfect in body and limbs.

waist, but older women and mothers were covered up, the latter carrying their babies tightly wrapped on their backs so as to leave their hands free for work in the fields or in their huts.

To judge from the number of small children, the birth-rate was high – and all the children seemed perfect in body and limbs. During our time in the village only one death occurred, and that from old age. 'Chippy', our ship's carpenter, made a coffin for him, their first.

Burial had of course to take place as soon as possible after death in that climate, and was usually in a simple cloth shroud. The whole village turned out for this special funeral and members of our crew acted as bearers. The ceremony, apparently a Christian one, was carried out, as far as I could tell, by a lay preacher instructed by missionaries. As we lowered the coffin, to our surprise all the people burst into 'Onward Christian Soldiers', beautifully sung in their own language. Whenever, today, I hear people singing the new national anthem of South Africa it takes me back to that sad day under the palm trees of Liberia's southern coast. And I remember the first words of our Christian saviours – 'We Christians' – and how these words were exemplified in the hospitality, kindness and friendship that they gave us.

The Chief and his elders maintained a strict code of conduct, and when my souvenir compass disappeared from my hut, and I reported this to the Chief, it was immediately returned. Every two or three days every family would carry out a foot inspection, and one day I joined it in order to find out why. To my surprise, a sand-tick was discovered and removed from the hard skin on the ball of my right foot: these insects are easily picked up and burrow under the skin to lay their eggs, so the inspections had a very practical purpose. Indeed, when I eventually reached home another tick had to be removed from the same foot and this time the whole area had become inflamed by the eggs laid there.

There was no prison in the village, but sanctions were available against those who broke its laws. Shortly after our arrival we noticed a man who spent all his time on the fringe of the bush, never entering the village. One day, out of curiosity, we approached him as we walked along the bush-path and he became frightened and attempted to run away, but kept falling over. When we got close enough we saw that a short, heavy log was manacled to his leg, so that he could move only with difficulty and by holding the heavy log up in both hands. He cowered away from us when we approached, evidently ashamed of himself and the punishment to which he had been sentenced for whatever crime it was that he had committed. We tried to find out about this, but nobody would answer our questions. No doubt this silence on the subject was an obligation under their law.

Another highlight of our time in Liberia was the wedding. Michael and I were sitting outside his hut in the main village, chatting over the past and speculating about the future. In the late afternoon the village was very quiet. Most of the domestic chores were completed in the morning and after this the women went off to cultivate their allotments. Now the silence was broken by laughter and the clapping of hands. Ten women, smartly dressed in bright garments and adorned with shell necklaces, had gathered outside one of the huts, where they performed a soft, shuffling dance. One of them was the bride-to-be, and at the end of the dance the hut's occupant came out and gave her a present. This ritual was repeated in turn at every hut in the village, and the bride's attendants were soon laden with gifts ranging from enamel plates and jugs to garden implements for working the allotments. It was a very happy occasion in which all of the villagers took a great interest and all of us were invited to attend the wedding feast the following day.

The wedding ceremony itself was private to the family and seems to have taken place in the mission hut; the feast was open to all and sundry and took place at sunset. We gathered around a large fire in the square, with the bride and groom in their place of honour next to the Chief. The main dish was roast goat, served with sweet potatoes, a very pleasant change for us after all those heads and tails of fish. Then there was singing and ritual dancing to which we contributed a rendering (somewhat late in the day) of 'Here Comes the Bride', followed by 'Calon Lân'. These were very well received and there were repeated requests for encores. The bride was radiant in her bright sari, with cowrie shells strung around her neck and ankles. The honeymoon must have been spent locally because I saw her working on her allotment the following day.

In spite of these highlights, time hung heavy on our hands. We maintained our watch, less hopeful each day that our signal would be noticed, and continued to debate ways of sending a message out. The best bet undoubtedly was to send volunteers northwards with village guides, but there could be no question of this until our condition had improved. The heat would be intense, the going rough – bush and soft sand – we had no shoes and travelling would be possible only during the oppressive daylight hours. It was, I considered, a brave man who would volunteer for such an attempt.

On 10 October, 1942 I was on morning beach-watch with four others, sitting apathetically in the shade near our palm-leaf S O S, casting a dull eye sea- and skyward from time to time. It was 11.45 a.m. Morning watch nearing its end.

Suddenly, the drone of an aircraft engine far away to the north-west. We ran out at once into the heavy sun of the open beach, vigorously waving palm fronds. The aircraft came imperceptibly into view, the lowest yet as to altitude, and the closest to shore. As it came closer, we could see that it was on a course south-easterly, parallel to shore and about a quarter of a mile out. Heart thumping, I sent one man off immediately to alert the village. The afternoon watch arrived to take over at noon.

Thank heaven! The aircraft was holding its course. Soon it was close enough for us to make out the R.A.F. markings. I whipped the scarf from around my waist and ran up and down, waving frantically. It passed by – but I knew we had been seen. It banked left, returned directly over our S O S and all our furiously waving village friends.

CHAPTER FIVE

The aircraft had descended to such a low altitude that we could see the pilot, waving back. It is impossible to describe our feeling of joy and relief; there were tears in our eyes as we looked forward to being rescued; everyone was waving and shouting. It circled, made a further sweep and dropped a small canister virtually at our feet. This contained the following message: 'Presume you are survivors. Stop. Reporting your sighting to Base Freetown. Stop. Will return in the morning with food supplies.' By the time we had read this the aircraft had returned to its patrol and was out of sight.

Nobody had much sleep that night and we were back on the beach, together with most of the villagers, by six o'clock the next morning. The children were as excited as we were and all eyes were turned to the north along the golden sandy foreshore and out over the white tops of the heavy breakers. How slowly time passes for impatient men! The hours dragged by and it was eleven o'clock and nothing had happened. We began to wonder whether the events of the previous day had really happened and re-read the pilot's message frequently to reassure ourselves. Only the children were cheerful now.

Midday passed, and still no sign of the aircraft. Then, faint and far away, the sound of engines and it reappeared, flying low and directly towards us. Another message was dropped: 'Clear beach for dropping area for food supplies'. The aircraft made two runs, dropping a large parachute container on each one. The first landed on target, the second in the top of a palm tree from which it was rescued in no time at all by excited young villagers.

When, in later life, I undertook the researches on which this account is based, I was able to obtain a copy of the log of Hudson T/200, operating from Freetown. It was crewed by Pilot Officers Johnston, Edwards and Thornton and Flight Sergeant Perry, and its daily patrols included wreck and convoy escort, anti-submarine sweeps, reconnaissance and searching for survivors. On 11 October the Operations Record Book contains the following information: 'Survivors seen on beach, food dropped at 12.33'.

The containers were carried shoulder-high into the village square and ceremoniously opened there by our senior officers. In an atmosphere reminiscent of Christmas morning, the contents were produced and identified one by one to the accompaniment of gasps and cheers. Each container was brim full of supplies: tinned butter, bacon, cheese, cans of meat, bread, beans, condensed milk and soup (can-openers not forgotten), coffee, sugar, biscuits, powdered milk and orange crystals. The mothers of the village, with exclamations of delight, examined the items in detail. The loaves of bread intrigued them – they had never seen such a product before. When we broke a loaf in half and offered small pieces of bread to mothers and children, their reaction was most interesting. With doubtful expressions on their faces, they first studied the loaf carefully, then cautiously raised their share to their lips, with their eyes all the time watching us eat. Finally they took the plunge and broad smiles and laughter confirmed that it was to their taste. One container included a message from the naval C. in C., Freetown, to the effect that a rescue vessel, HMS *Spaniard*, was on its way and should reach us within forty-eight hours.

The chief officer invited the whole village to join us for supper that evening and we had a right royal Afro-European feast: fresh fish-heads and tails, minestrone soup with hunks of bread, cheese and biscuits, fresh coffee or orange juice, bananas and coconuts. For us survivors, who had seen no British food since the explosion, it was everything the Ritz could have supplied apart from silver cutlery and a Havana with the coffee. The banquet concluded with a singsong around the fire, hands linked in friendship, the whole happy occasion rounded off with the villagers' favourite hymn, 'Onward, Christian Soldiers'.

Next day dawned with everyone in high spirits, anticipating the arrival of HMS *Spaniard*. We spent the whole day on or close to the beach, with frequent glances to the north. Now only the children were sad. We had been a novelty to them, personal friends on first-name terms – and they would dearly have liked us to stay.

At sunset there was a second banquet. The guest-list had increased dramatically because word had spread through the bush that free meals were on offer at our village. The visitors arrived with big gleaming smiles and hands outstretched in greeting, and they were very welcome to share what ought to be our final night there. As I returned to my accommodation, however, I was aware of a heightened temperature coupled with nausea – which I put down to over-excitement and over-eating.

Next morning I awoke shivering, but this had subsided by sunrise. Malaria, I thought, not greatly perturbed because very soon I should be aboard HMS *Spaniard* and receiving professional medical treatment. My two shipmates left early for the main village, but I stayed behind in bed, requesting them to advise the Senior Officer that I was ill. About 11 a.m. Michael arrived with one or two friends to see how I was, but by then I was feeling much better – no fever, only the familiar pain in foot and thigh.

We were all happily chatting when Michael's host, Josiah, arrived excited and panting, having run all the way with the news: 'Massa Mike, battleship arrive!' My pain disappeared as if by magic, I collected my belongings (one lifeboat compass), made my farewells and was presented by the children with a model canoe. The others set off at a run for the beach, something quite beyond me in the midday heat even though I was longing to see the 'battleship'. Michael stayed behind and helped me to complete the quarter-mile walk.

As we emerged from the trees we got our first glimpse of HMS *Spaniard*, at anchor two miles from shore, well clear of the heavy breakers. Our saviour was no battleship, but a Hull/Grimsby trawler seconded to the Admiralty and converted for minesweeping. She carried two 'jolly boats' (long boats with square sterns), but her captain was unwilling to risk them in the breakers and advised our senior officer, by morse lamp, to come out by canoe to discuss rescue procedures, in particular the problem of stretcher-cases and walking wounded.

An urgent meeting was convened and the senior officer agreed to proceed to HMS *Spaniard* together with a senior representative from the village. It was further agreed that when she was ready to receive us she would hoist the red and yellow international code flag 'Y' (indicating 'Yes'). The senior officer was taking no chances and put on his life-jacket before boarding the canoe. It was launched in the usual way with the assistance of men standing chest-high in the water and we settled down for a long wait, wondering whether he would survive the rough ride. We watched the canoe, its occupants paddling furiously, dip into, then ride over the white foam and spray, but its motion was so violent that he was thrown out and washed ashore, while the canoe remained upright and returned to the beach to the accompaniment of hearty laughter from the spectators. We could not appreciate this maritime comedy of errors, being conscious – in my case particularly so on account of my injury – that we would have to survive a similar ordeal if we were to reach the *Spaniard*.

Before a second attempt was made, the senior officer received a briefing on how to retain his balance and it was decided to move farther down the beach. This time, although the passage was no less rough, everyone survived the rollers and cheers arose on shore. Our own rescue could proceed as soon as the 'Y' flag was displayed – every fisherman in the village had volunteered to take one survivor in his canoe and we were delighted to accept the offer.

Now it was time to say goodbye to our saviours and friends and, anxious as we all were to be away, every one of us was very sad to leave such kind, loving Christian people. I was already in tears before the handshaking and embracing began, conscious that it was extremely unlikely that we would meet again. Ever since then I have looked out for news of Liberia and was distressed to learn of the unrest between 1992 and 1996, wondering if our happy young friends, in their late middle age by then, had survived.

My host had instructed me carefully on how to observe the balancing procedure in a dug-out canoe, but I was terrified among the rollers and clung on in a central position. Once through them it was smooth canoeing all the way out and I kept my eyes fixed on the *Spaniard*, not being able to bear to look back to the villagers waving on the beach. We headed for the Jacob's Ladder and as we drew closer it became clear that this was one vessel to which the term 'rust-bucket' might fairly be applied – hull and superstructure alike were heavily streaked. There was no time, at this crisis of the war, for painting or anything but essential maintenance, and HMS *Spaniard* was a very busy unit of H.M. Naval Forces, indispensable as an inshore support vessel at Freetown. Handsome is as handsome does!

When we came alongside it became clear that a heavy swell was running. I was seized by two burly A.B.s and hauled abruptly out of the canoe, clinging to my compass and model boat. The moment I reached the deck a cigarette was stuck into my mouth and a strong tot of Navy Rum thrust into my hand – much appreciated in spite of my being a non-smoker and, under the rules of my cadetship, a total abstainer!

There had been no further upsets and soon all of us were gathered safely on deck to be greeted by the commander. Immediately thereafter we were lined up in front of a Royal Navy cameraman for official photographs. HMS *Spaniard* weighed anchor with thirty canoes in attendance, their occupants waving a friendly farewell. They were given three long blasts on the ship's steam whistle as she headed seaward on passage to Marshall, the port of the U.S. airfield. 16.00 hours, 12 October 1942.

Slowly our jungle home and friends of nine long days receded astern and we began to adjust ourselves to yet another way of life. On this small ship, accommodation was scanty and cramped – under an awning on the fore-deck. We had been steaming for no more than an hour and a half when action stations was called and hands prepared to launch depth-charges: sonar had detected an enemy submarine. Surely we were not going to be torpedoed again? Two full-speed attacks were made, the depth-charges sending mushrooms of water high astern, before the intercom announced that the contact had been a false one. A shame, thought the commander, to leave all those dead and stunned fish floating, so he ordered a celebratory fish-and-chip supper and launched one of the jolly boats. I volunteered to help man it and am prominent in the photograph on p. 78, helping to unload the large 'catch'.

The supper, which I very much enjoyed, is one of my last clear memories for some days. I recollect that it was a cold night and that I chose to turn in on a mess deck table rather than the open deck, and I also remember arriving at Marshall next morning and being transferred to a fast ML 290 Torpedo Boat. Then I collapsed into semi-consciousness with malaria and have no memory of arriving at Freetown at 13.30 on 14 October.

When I came to I was in a warm, comfortable bed in the sick-bay of the armed Cruiser, HMS *Carnarvon Castle*. I had been delirious for forty-eight hours, yet nobody else had been affected. Why me? I wondered. My leg was heavily bandaged and hoisted up high, and the medical team was much more concerned about its condition than about the malaria. The infection had spread up to my thigh, the doctor explained, and a painful procedure must be started at once if it was to be saved.

He was as good as his word. Now that I was fully conscious the wound was treated with a very hot poultice, padded and tightly bandaged. They told me to bear the agonising pulsation of the wound to the limit of my tolerance, and I took a tight hold on the arm of the male nurse. The pain beat like a large drum all down my leg and the

HMS *Spaniard*. Recovering boat laden with fish after dropping depth charge.
Author is facing camera.

HMS *Spaniard*. Survivors being addressed by the Commander.
Author with arms folded and heavy beard.

nurse held the bandages tightly until I was about to scream. Then they were rapidly released and a large plug of the poultice shot out bringing with it a mass of stinking pus which had drained from the infected area and an immediate sensation of relief. But the same procedure had to be repeated day and night while, incidentally, I recovered from the malaria.

Michael, who visited me every day, explained that I had collapsed on the torpedo boat and that nobody had known what was wrong or how to revive me. Someone had said that I was only suffering from malaria and should be wrapped in blankets and kept warm. As the boat travelled at high speed and its motion was quite violent, I was strapped down to a bench beneath the port torpedo tube. I had a raging temperature and was sweating profusely, but, thank heaven, knew nothing of it. He also told me that, on arrival at Freetown, there had been a quick identity check and that everyone was then fitted out with a suit, shirt, socks, shoes and so on. The *Carnarvon Castle* was lying at anchor in the bay and we embarked in company with hundreds of other survivors of the slaughter which was continuing among shipping on passage from the South Atlantic to Freetown now that Dönitz, having accepted defeat in the North Atlantic, had switched his U-boats to this poorly defended area.

It was at Freetown that the survivors of the *Quebec City* were reunited and we learned what had happened to our other lifeboat. Twelve days after our separation they were sighted by a Spanish freighter, which offered to take them on board. As Spain was neutral, our captain had opted for food and water and obtained his position, which turned out to be three days from landfall. However, while still alongside the Spanish vessel, they were sighted by a Royal Navy patrol frigate and rescued.

The captain had reported the position at which his ship had been torpedoed and the frigate immediately set course to the south-west in search of our lifeboat (the captain was convinced that we were astern of him because he believed that his lifeboat had been handled better and achieved a better daily average: he could not know that our additional area of sail and spinnaker had put us a day and a half ahead). The frigate had returned to the position of sinking on a zigzag course, using our colleagues as additional lookouts to maintain a 360° scan. Freetown naval base had been informed that survivors had been picked up and that one lifeboat was missing

My passage home was tedious and long. Day after day I languished in the sick bay, envying my fellow survivors their first-class passenger accommodation. But it was no pleasure cruise for them either – the dining-room had to have carefully staggered sittings to cope with feeding 2,500 people. Of these 1,200 were survivors and the rest R.A.F. and naval personnel. There was very little deck space free for any kind of exercise. Michael visited me every day and kept me informed of what was going on, but he was my only visitor. As far as the rest of my shipmates were concerned it was, it seems, a case of 'I'm all right, Jack!' Total war leaves little room for the airs and graces of civilised life.

Michael told me that our course was first westerly for several days, then north-westerly, well out towards the middle of the North Atlantic, before we turned north, then north-east for Northern Ireland and the Clyde. Two days before we reached the Tail of the Bank, Greenock, all the walking wounded were discharged from sick bay and moved into passenger accommodation. My left foot was bandaged and given a padded heel for walking on: the open wound was clean now, and healing rapidly. I was given a suit of rough tweed, one khaki shirt, one pair of stockings, one pair of brown shoes and one razor. For forty days I had been a stateless person with no identification other than the word of the senior officer, but now immigration staff issued me with an identity card and landing permit. In addition I received one month's food-ration coupons and sufficient clothing coupons for the purchase of replacements for my lost uniforms, other clothing, shoes and accessories.

I dressed cautiously and clumsily. After going naked for so long, a shirt and suit felt very strange. The latter, moreover, had the texture of rough, pliable cardboard. My appearance at dinner that night was distinctly forlorn: I wore only one shoe, my left leg was heavily bandaged, my weight was down to nine stone and the shaving off of my beard had left most of my face greyish-white, in sharp contrast to the rough, sore, sunburned skin all around it.

16.00 hours. 29 October 1942. At anchor at the Tail of the Bank, awaiting disembarkation orders. Tugs and launches bustled and fussed around us. At 20.00 came an announcement: 'Attention, all survivors. Disembarkation will commence at 18.00 hours tomorrow, Friday. You are required to present yourself immediately after breakfast with your identity card and landing permit. Rail travel warrants will then be issued, and you will receive £3 to assist with subsistence.'

Friday was a long and frustrating day. We stood in queues for hours on end. Two thousand men had to be questioned individually about where they lived and their nearest railway station and to sign three official forms before they could receive their warrant and £3. It takes more than a world war to wipe out bureaucracy! It was 19.00 before we began disembarking, on a dark night, in blackout conditions, onto Clyde ferries. These conveyed us to Greenock Pier where we boarded special trains for Glasgow Central Station, where we arrived at 22.00. The station was under armed guard and civilian passengers barred from its forecourt and platforms. Five special trains had been laid on – for the Midlands, East Coast, London, West Coast and Wales/South West respectively – and we were escorted to our places by army personnel.

Michael, bound for Cambridge, was assigned to the London train, so we made our farewells before boarding and promised to maintain our friendship. (It was to last for fifty-four years. After our parting he progressed steadily, achieved his command and held it until retirement. He proved to be a great seaman and a fine leader, and we corresponded regularly, though we met on only three occasions, each time to celebrate our survival of what he had christened 'The Big Bang of 19 September 1942'. I lost a very dear friend when he died suddenly of a heart attack in 1996.)

The scene on Glasgow Central Station was like a black-and-white war film. Under close army supervision, the first to be loaded were the stretcher-cases. Then the walking wounded, myself among them. The women of the WVS and Red Cross were everywhere, helping us to board our trains, ensuring that we were as comfortable as possible, offering cups of tea. It was midnight by now and word came through that the Luftwaffe had been bombing the sidings in the East Kilbride area and all rail movement had been suspended. It was 01.30 before my train eventually moved out.

My initial destination was Crewe, where I had to change for Newport, Cardiff and Swansea. There were frequent stoppages and long delays due to enemy raids on cities and towns along our route. I reached Swansea at 16.00 on Sunday 1 November, forty-five hours after disembarkation. I was totally exhausted, frustrated by my lack of mobility, and I had barely enough cash left in my pocket for a taxi home. There was, of course, nobody to welcome me – my mother had no idea even that I had reached Scotland. I stood there at the taxi-rank, weary and dishevelled in my creased blue suit, one brown shoe protruding from my pocket. Two cabs were in service, but, not surprisingly in the circumstances, their drivers ignored me – apart from my unprepossessing appearance, I had no luggage, not even a carrier-bag. All my worldly goods were the crumpled clothes I stood up in, one lifeboat compass (secondhand) and one model canoe (Liberian).

I hobbled over to one of the taxis and asked the price of my fare home. Even after I had proved that I had the money, the driver remained suspicious of me because war-time travellers always had their belongings with them. When we reached my home, and I had paid the fare, the taxi moved off very slowly, its driver looking back several times as he continued to wonder who I was and where I had come from. If he should happen to read this story, and has not forgotten the mysterious passenger he picked up at High Street Station nearly sixty years ago, his curiosity will now be satisfied.

I knocked at the front door and was greeted by an outburst of barking from my great pal, Shaun, a twelve-year-old Pembrokeshire corgi. As soon as she reached the door she picked up my scent and the barking was replaced with a high-pitched yowl of excitement. When Mother opened the door the dog leapt into my arms, almost knocking me over. Mother was not one for showing her emotions in public, but the sight of my strange, gaunt and bedraggled figure overcame her inhibitions and she threw her arms around me and Shaun and hugged us both together.

My brother was away in the army, and my sister with the Red Cross, so I had plenty of opportunity to enjoy being at home again. A happy home is always with us when we are away from it, most of all when we are in danger and uncertain whether we shall survive to see it again. How many times had I given it up for lost? When I was trapped by the explosion; as we all stood waiting for the torpedo that was to administer the *coup de grâce*; as the U-boat circled and drew closer; hungry and thirsty in the open boat; facing the breakers, waiting for rescue, all the way through the long journey home – even on the railway journey, under threat from bombing. There was an overwhelming sense of relief to be back in this safe, familiar place and feel the long tensions slip away.

I now learned how news had reached the outside world about the torpedoing of the *Quebec City*. When our second lifeboat was rescued, Freetown was informed of the ship's name and that another lifeboat was unaccounted for. On 12 October 1942, my mother received a letter from the authorities:

> We regret to inform you that the vessel in which your son was serving has been lost by enemy action. Two lifeboats were safely launched and one was duly picked up, but we have no news of the second boat, in which your son left the vessel. In all probability the survivors have been rescued by a passing vessel and there can be no further news until that vessel reaches port. You may rest assured that immediately we have this good news we shall pass it on to you.

So she hoped, and waited, and suffered in silence like so many next of kin in Britain, Germany and elsewhere. Our minister, I learned many years later, had walked two miles every day to enquire if she had received further news, and to comfort her. On 20 October the telegram arrived (and it is not hard to imagine what thoughts and feelings she endured as she opened it – or enjoyed after she had read it):

> SON SAFE AND WELL STOP ALL MEMBERS OF SECOND LIFEBOAT ARE SAFE AND WELL STOP ARRANGEMENTS WILL BE MADE SHORTLY FOR THEIR RETURN TO THIS COUNTRY

The author on leave, at 16 years of age.

'Our gallant men entertained by the Minister of Labour . . .

. . . and Jessie Matthews.'

After a good rest and some home-cooking that was extremely acceptable in spite of meagre war-time rations, I reported to our family doctor, who suggested that I attend Morriston Military Hospital. This was a new construction, rapidly assembled out of breeze-blocks and prefabricated buildings. When the doctor was examining me, I complained of soreness in the ball of my foot and when the hard skin was cut away they discovered the sand-tick that I had brought back from the Liberian beach. I had entirely recovered from the malaria, and was to experience no recurrence. No more ticks, either.

My career had in fact been advanced by the sinking of my ship. By government decree, any cadet who had survived three years active foreign service was granted remission of one year of the four-year requirement. This had become necessary because so many young officers had been lost and must be replaced as rapidly as possible. I attended the Sir John Cass marine section of London University to study for my first Board of Trade qualifying examination. One day, in January 1943, a lecture on correction procedures for the standard magnetic compass was abruptly interrupted by the head of Navigation Studies. He had received a telephone call from the House of Commons requesting the attendance of two officers in uniform at a reception arranged by the Minister of Labour (his ministry included war transport), Ernest Bevin, at the Allied Forces Club in Piccadilly. It was a typical war-time propaganda exercise, with glamour supplied by Miss Jessie Matthews and other stars of the era and a speech by the Minister praising the hard work and gallantry of those involved in the Battle of the Atlantic. A colleague and I were chosen because we happened to have our uniforms within easy reach, and we enjoyed the break from study and the excellent meal – a welcome change from wartime rations. Our photographs appeared in the papers next day under the caption:

OUR GALLANT MEN OF THE BATTLE OF THE ATLANTIC
ENTERTAINED BY MINISTER OF LABOUR.

You can well imagine the comments of our fellow students when we returned to our studies!

After three months' intensive study I passed the examination and achieved the status of an officer and my first gold braid stripe. I was appointed third officer of the SS *Anglo African*, then being re-fitted at

Barrow-in-Furness and modified to land assault forces and military supplies on invasion beaches.

As soon as the re-fit had been completed we proceeded to Liverpool, where we loaded newly-printed Allied banknotes for use after the invasion of North Africa, then set sail for North Africa and the Mediterranean campaign, where I served for eighteen months and was promoted navigator/gunnery officer on the demise of a senior colleague. Initially, we were involved with the Indian Army Cavalry Mule Division, an unusual formation of which most people know nothing in spite of the important part it played in fighting over rough terrain.

Our function was to deliver mule pack divisions to beach-heads as close as possible to the action in which they were to take part. In combination with their officers and other ranks, we trained to achieve rapid and efficient landings, from as close to shore as possible, of up to 200 mules and 150 men. The process began in the eastern Mediterranean. Untrained mules were shipped down from eastern Turkey, Syria and north Lebanon to the naval base at Beirut. Inland from the port is a range of beautiful mountains, often snow-capped even when the coast is basking in hot sunshine. Among these mountains the mules were trained, under conditions as close to those of real combat as possible. They worked in teams of twelve, each of which contained a leading mule which the rest would follow, in the sea or on land. When the animals had been mountain-trained we carried out marine exercises in which they would be offloaded close to shore and swim for the beach under simulated gunfire with an Indian Army sergeant riding each leader.

As soon as the C.O., a full colonel, was satisfied that his company was fully trained and ready for action, we would embark a contingent of troops, mules and equipment and proceed to a predetermined rendezvous, usually Taranto on the heel of Italy. We were then assigned a beach-head and escorted there by a small combined naval escort which provided concentrated ack-ack cover against air attack and suitable protection from enemy naval craft.

The Indian troops had so perfected beach-head operations that they could complete one in a period of sixteen hours non-stop, day-and-night activity. Each mule was led from its pen to a point directly below the centre of a hatchway. There a special harness known as a canvas belly-band was strapped on and cinched with a steel clamp

The veterinary surgeons of the Indian Mule Division,
the Adriatic, Christmas Day, 1944.

Captain Caradog Thomas with the ship's mascot 'Margaret'.

Indian Mule Division, Adriatic, 1944, with the ship's mascot 'Margaret'.

Captain Caradog Thomas, ship's officers and Army vets,
Indian Mule Division Crew, 1944.

known as a senhouse slip, which was attached to the winch runner wire hook so that the animal could be hoisted out of the hold and lowered into the sea. There the sergeant riding the leading mule would release it. I was astonished at the behaviour of the mules and also of the officers' horses, all of which seemed to relish swimming. Some mules, however, would wander from the pack – on one occasion I spotted three of them heading straight out to the open sea – and we had small, fast launches to round them up when this occurred. As soon as the landing was completed we departed the scene as quickly as we could for Beirut, running the gauntlet of enemy air attacks from bases in Greece, Crete and Cyprus, to repeat the process.

The Indian Division was engaged on the Adriatic and eastern coastline of Italy, from Brindisi northward, and played a particularly distinguished part in the assault on Monte Cassino. Here the German

As navigating officer with my quartermaster.

(left and below)
As navigating officer.

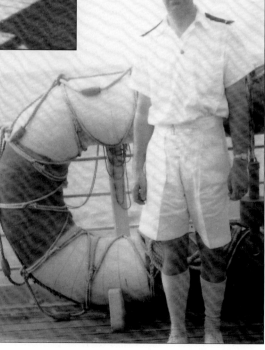

army, from a commanding position high up on the mountain, held up the Allied advance for a long time. The terrain was so rugged that only the sure-footed mule companies were able to scale it with any ease, and they brought up heavy guns and supplies under heavy German gunfire.

We were twice seconded to the U.S. Cavalry (Texas Rangers Division) whose colourful uniform included jodhpurs, highly-polished boots and six-shooters on both hips. They were acting in support of U.S. troops on the west of the Italian mainland and although their appearance brought Western movies to mind, they were brave fighters and accomplished horsemen.

As the Allied advance continued the Germans fell back to a strong defence line north of Rome and my ship was assigned to the blockade of Corsica and Sardinia. Here we became involved with the Italian cavalry when Corsica surrendered. This time our task was to ship these crack Alpine troops back to the mainland to join forces with the Allies. I was surprised, on the day of embarkation, to see that, in spite of several months of blockade, the officers and men marching along the quay were extremely smart. They wore full-dress uniform which included alpine hats with large curling feathers protruding from the left-hand side. Once they were aboard it was my job to liaise with the Italian officers to organise shipboard routine and safety drills. I found both officers and men very friendly but disinclined for action against the Germans: many of them hoped to be classified as prisoners-of-war when they landed at Civitavecchia, the port of Rome.

One of their senior officers presented me with his Beretta pistol as a keepsake and token of friendship, but I handed it in at my local police station during an amnesty on guns. The men too were for the most part friendly, especially on the morning inspections when they stood to attention alongside their horses or mules on the horse deck. The stables were mucked-out twice a day, and then they would sing their favourite arias in true Italian style, happy, no doubt, to be at long last on their way back home to their wives and families.

When we reached Civitavecchia we were able to berth alongside in spite of the destruction of the port facilities by heavy bombing. I managed a quick visit to the town, which was also badly damaged. However, I came across a ruined church and found, amid the debris of walls and towers, an intact altar with a large golden cross and two supporting candlesticks. The candles had been lit and many local people were kneeling before them in prayer. When I regained the quay I found the Italian troops all smiles. They had rescued six porcelain baths from wrecked houses in the neighbourhood, filled them with fresh water and their horses and mules were contentedly drinking their fill.

Our final mission in the Mediterranean involved secondment to the Free French. We proceeded to Bastia on the north-east coast of Corsica to prepare for the invasion of southern France. Captain and senior officers, of whom I was now one, went ashore to be briefed about the embarkation of French troops from North Africa, the Gooms. These men, all of them six feet tall, and with tribal markings incised on their cheeks, were renowned as fierce fighters. Their uniform was unusual to say the least, an ankle-length gown rather like a nightshirt. They were fanatically loyal to their French superiors and fiercely protective towards the French nurses who tended their wounds during and after skirmishes with the enemy.

Our entry into the port of Marseilles frightened me more than any other war experience, not because of enemy fire, but the weather conditions. There was only one safe route, directed by the mine-sweeping flotilla which swept ahead of us. Unfortunately, the Mistral had been blowing steadily for forty-eight hours, raising a steep, choppy sea, and our true course was beam on to this. Once committed to our entry run we could not deviate at all because of the surrounding minefield.

My ship was riding high because we had no solid bottom-weight cargo, only troops, horses and mules accommodated high above the water-line. There was excessive rolling which made most of the men seasick, though they stood resolutely by their animals, trying to calm them. In spite of their best efforts, many horses and mules became frightened and kicked out, destroying the horseboxes, which collapsed around them. Many horses on the upper deck simply vanished over the side during rolls of up to 35°. Had this been an assault landing it would have been a disastrous failure.

Our first glimpse of occupied France was a harbour badly damaged by the retreating German army. Quayside cranes had been blown up and were leaning precariously over the side. Once the soldiers and their animals were safely ashore, though, we were rewarded with the luxury of a whole night of peace, under no threat of enemy attack and able to go to bed free of our oppressive, necessary bosom companion, the life-jacket. After four years of conflict, apprehension and steaming into the unknown this was utter bliss.

The following morning I witnessed a disturbing incident on the quay. During the night the harbour area had been made completely secure by the Military Police and turned into a holding-pen for captured rearguard German soldiers. Apparently content that, for them, the war was over, they were well-behaved and sat in groups, chatting to their guards. Not far away, everything was in turmoil. Resistance forces had rounded up known collaborators, male and female, and, to the accompaniment of screaming and shouting, were shaving the women's heads. The Military Police would not interfere between the Resistance and their own nationals, but when they had finished, all the prisoners, German and French alike, were locked up together in a spacious cargo transit shed.

Our final mission, a peaceful one, was the delivery to Civitavecchia of four beautiful white horses for ceremonial parades. These animals each had a personal soldier groom in attendance, together with an army vet. Apparently, preparations were being made for a grand Victory Parade through Rome. Later I read about this and saw in my newspaper a picture of one of the white horses leading it with the C. in C. British Forces, General Sir Maitland Wilson ('Tubby' to the troops) in the saddle.

With the establishment of peace in the western hemisphere we returned to the United Kingdom. Remembering, as I often had during my subsequent service, the torpedoing of the *Quebec City* and my narrow escape from death, I thought with profound admiration and gratitude of the men who had fought the Battle of the Atlantic. Friend and foe alike had shown skill, endurance, courage and tenacity, contending not only with each other, but with winter storms and mountainous seas. Their warfare with and on the sea had demanded sacrifices far beyond any call of duty, and taken the lives of so many. I thought of the Sailors' Prayer:

> O Lord, have mercy upon my ship,
> Thy ocean so large, my ship so small,
> In your mercy, take care of us all.

And I thought also, yet again, of the enemy who had been my friend, the captain of U-156, and wondered what had been his fate. I told myself that, one day, if it were possible, I would find out.

CHAPTER SIX

With peace re-established, I applied, in 1945, for a position with a major international shipping line and was appointed fourth officer (one gold stripe – a loss of two from with my wartime grade). After the formative experiences of war, peacetime service aboard passenger-carrying vessels brought insight into a very different world in which I travelled extensively and met a variety of interesting people, some of them very well known.

As a very young officer I had my first experience of a hurricane, and, unusually, it was an amusing one. After a very strenuous night at bridge watch stations, the ship's motion at times so violent that she appeared almost to stand on her head, we at last gained the eye of the storm. Astern of us was a quite phenomenal sight: the heavy black overcast of low cloud was raised up, as if someone was lifting a curtain, to reveal the rising sun and a glimmer of blue sky. The captain was so struck by this that he decided it must be recorded, and sent me to find a keen amateur photographer among the passengers.

This photographer was, in real life, a bishop and had spent the night in the main passenger lounge offering comfort to distressed passengers and their families in fear for their lives. 'Ask the bishop if he will be kind enough to join me on the bridge, with his camera,' the captain ordered.

I was fully clothed, of course, in oilskins, sou'wester and seaboots, and I was wet from top to toe with salt spray, but it is not for a junior officer to question his captain's wishes. I threaded my way through the frightened, tearful, seasick huddle, found the bishop and whispered the captain's message into his ear. My appearance, and the fact that I was whispering, convinced them that their end was imminent and it was immediately obvious that I had got to do something about it. Thus it was that I made my first speech to assembled passengers, assuring them that there was nothing whatever to worry about. When they learned that the bishop was going to the bridge to take a photograph rather than to administer the last rites, smiles broke out and calm was restored.

There was no time, as these early years went by, to reflect on wartime experiences – I was far too busy at my studies, achieving additional qualifications and working my way through the ranks. At the age of twenty-nine I obtained command, and although I remained at sea for only a year or two thereafter, I was lucky enough to enjoy a number of particularly interesting experiences.

Working my way through the ranks: Chief Officer c. 1950.

Gerald Durrell's well-known book, *The Overloaded Ark*, begins as follows: 'The ship nosed its way through the morning mist, across a sea as smooth as milk. A faint and exciting smell came to us from the invisible shore . . . and gradually the bay and the coastline came into view and gave me my first glimpse of Africa.' The ship was my ship, and in his 'Author's Acknowledgements' Mr Durrell was kind enough to mention 'the captain and crew of the ship . . . who did their utmost to make our voyage easy'. We carried him and his team to the British Cameroons (now the Republic of Cameroon), just north of what was at that time the Belgian Congo, and two months later we carried them back home with their collection of large and small wild animals.

Gerald Durrell is a great story-teller, but there is one story omitted from his book. It concerns our ship's cat, a large, overfed, one-eyed ginger tom named (it is hardly necessary to say) Nelson. Nelson was an inquisitive animal, and he was intrigued by the strange and much larger cats in Mr Durrell's collection. The first time he ventured near their cages, however, they flung themselves, snarling, against the bars and, as only a cat can, Nelson did a rapid double somersault and disappeared at high speed for the safety of the bridge deck. This happened several more times, but Nelson learned from experience that he was in no danger and took to making a daily nonchalant survey of his bigger brothers, who continued to react furiously. It was a leopard who suffered most from this teasing: each morning Nelson would saunter by, then settle down near the cage, while the leopard, furious at being defied by his strange one-eyed relation, growled and rattled his bars. Nelson lived to a ripe old age!

A completely contrasting voyage to the Cameroons brought back childhood memories of the *John Williams IV*, when I had the great pleasure of conveying a Roman Catholic mother general and twelve nuns on their way to service at a leper colony high on the slopes of Mount Cameroon. A captain is never able to spend much time away from his ship, but before this voyage began the mother general had invited me to spend a night at the mission, and I was very happy to do so.

Transport was a problem, but both the port authorities at Victoria and Fyffe's Banana Company were very helpful. The company operated a narrow-gauge railway through their plantations, which extended a considerable distance towards Mount Cameroon, and we travelled on an open, flat-topped banana wagon. What a picture! The mother general and her twelve nuns dressed from head to toe in full white habits, and Captain Jones in tropical uniform – all of them seated on clean banana leaves spread over the low-slung 'carriage'. Baboons were abundant in the dense plantations. They are vicious animals, though generally they keep their distance, but also rather amusing, for they mimic the actions of human beings. They kept a close eye on these strange invaders of their territory, running out onto the track as soon as we had passed, to see what we were up to. There was also a herd of African elephants, a menace to the tender trees, which they were liable to trample down.

The railway took us as far as the foot of the mountain, and there we were met by a party from the mission with mules to carry the nuns' luggage and other packages. We proceeded on foot along a well-worn path and I was conscious of an earlier walk along a smilar path under very different circumstances (sartorial ones included) and of how unsuitable my uniform was for such a setting. Every time I asked how much further we had to walk, the mother general teased me with a reminder that the silver-backed gorilla was very common in those parts. Had it not been for my interest in seeing the colony and my reluctance to lose face, I would have been happy to retreat.

When we reached our goal I was reminded again of my stay in the Liberian village because the colony's huts were identical. The church, however, and the nuns' accommodation were of wood, with corrugated iron roofs. I was given a rapid conducted tour before darkness closed in and, after dinner, was escorted to a bamboo hut on the fringe of the compound and left there with my thoughts and the light of a flickering oil-lamp which cast strange, wild shadows. Outside, the eerie, high-pitched whine of crickets and the bass croaking of jungle frogs. I thought of silver-backed gorillas and crossed my fingers.

However, the long night passed without incident, though it was nearly daybreak before I managed to sleep and almost at once I was awakened by the church and school bells. The day began with prayers at 6 a.m., followed by school at seven. I was deeply touched by the warm welcome I received from children and adults alike – they made me feel like a guest of honour and I treasure the memory. When I got back to my ship I sent my thanks in the form of a selection of canned foods to supplement the mission's own supplies. I have experienced evil and good in the course of a long life, and high among the examples of good is the devoted activity of those brave and dedicated young volunteer nuns.

It was company policy that, on every Sunday morning at sea, an inter-denominational church service should be held. This took place in the main lounge and was very popular, especially with the passengers, who often complimented me on my part in it as I made my way, afterwards, to the bridge for the morning meeting with my officers. My early chapel experience obviously stood me in good stead – I was well accustomed to standing at the lectern – and to this was added a deep and penetrating voice (very useful to a captain as to a minister!). One service, however, did not go quite according to plan.

We had encountered rough weather during the night, a moderate quarterly sea was running and the ship was rolling considerably. I discussed with the the senior purser the desirability of cancelling the service, but he said that most of the passengers would be upset if I did; so, at five minutes to eleven, I duly marched, at the head of my officers, all of us immaculate in full white tropical uniform, into the main lounge. An essential feature of the service was the grand piano which stood immediately in front of the congregation.

All went well at first, but as I announced the second hymn I noticed, through the lounge window, a rogue heavy swell, fast approaching. The congregation rose to their feet, the pianist struck up the opening verse and, simultaneously, the swell struck the ship. The congregation collapsed like a pack of cards. They quickly recovered, however, and scrambled back to their feet, determined to proceed with the hymn. They had barely begun when another heavy swell struck. This time they were prepared and managed, with a contortion or two, to maintain their balance. The pianist was not so fortunate: his instrument became unhooked from its anchor-stops and careered across the room, leaving him sitting there, open-mouthed. The service ended immediately. God must have appreciated our devotion, for nobody was even slightly injured.

Another potentially dangerous mishap occurred on passage from the Caribbean, when the ship shed her propellor. Luckily the weather was calm on this occasion, and there was no damage to the hull. Salvage tugs came out to us from the Azores and towed us to Lisbon for repairs and the shipping of a new screw. This time the passengers were delighted – they got five extra days free and sightseeing in Lisbon as well.

The captain of a ship has to be prepared for many eventualities. Part of the film, *Fire down Below*, released in 1957, was shot aboard my ship in Trinidad, and I met Rita Hayworth and Robert Mitchum. Another show-business experience was meeting Mary Martin, star of the musical *South Pacific*, on her way to Jamaica for a well-earned vacation following a two-year run in the West End. Miss Martin joined my ship shortly after completing her final performance and, on her last night aboard, entertained passengers and crew with excerpts from the show.

I met many other celebrities during my short period of command. In my day, cricket teams travelled by sea, and I carried the Duke of

Norfolk's Eleven, Tom Graveney, Willie Watson, Freddie Trueman and David Sheppard (later Bishop of Liverpool) among them, to their tour of the West Indies. They were extremely smart in grey flannels and blazers bearing a crowned letter N on the pocket. A match was played between a ship's team and the tourists and our passengers were amused and delighted to see the ship's cricketers win. We had an unfair advantage in our superior knowledge of conditions: the match was played with a ball made of rope wound round a steel nut and soaked in salt water and they never came to terms with the unpredictable spin which it took from the teak deck!

The governors of Barbados, Trinidad, Jamaica and Bermuda travelled by my ship, as did Princess Alice, Countess of Athlone, vice-president of the University of Jamaica. Invariably accompanied by a German maid of honour who had served her for fifty years, she was accorded all the pomp and circumstance of royalty. I remember, on one occasion, joining the Governor of Trinidad in escorting Her Royal Highness, followed, as always, by her maid, down the gangway to the accompaniment of the Trinidad military band. All the local dignitaries were lined up to receive the royal handshake – and they shook hands with equal enthusiasm with the maid, who received their greeting in a suitably regal manner!

We carried some interesting cargoes also, in my time. In those days turtle soup was always served at the Lord Mayor's banquet, and it was we who loaded the turtles, live, at the Turks and Caicos Islands and conveyed them in specially-constructed canvas 'tanks' whose sea-water was changed every day. When we reached the U.K., the turtles went to Billingsgate in readiness for the banquet. This trade has now ceased, the turtle being a protected species.

Undoubtedly, my strangest experience in command occurred on a voyage home from the Cameroons. New Year was always celebrated with a dinner-dance, and among our passengers was a doctor, travelling with his wife. They attended the dance, and next morning he reported to me that his wife had contracted smallpox and said that she must be kept in quarantine in their accommodation and that nobody must come into contact with her. But she had mixed freely with the other passengers at the dance and a number of the men had danced with her, so I had to alert the port authority at Liverpool where, as a precautionary measure, dock-workers had to undergo emergency vaccination. We stopped at the Mersey Bar and staff from the Department of Tropical Diseases came aboard, conducted a thorough examination and tests, and found that the woman did not have smallpox. Imagine my feelings when, with many people nursing sore arms, I reported next day to my marine superintendent! On his advice, I departed quickly and very quietly and had already left Lime Street Station before the Press began besieging my ship for an interview. That is not the end of the story, though. There *was* something wrong with the doctor's wife: he had made an attempt to murder her. He was arrested and later convicted.

After two years in command of ocean-going passenger and cargo liners I was, in 1955, at the age of thirty-one, selected by the board of directors for command of a desk ashore, a major promotion to marine superintendent. My life was transformed: from the command of one ship I progressed in due course to responsibility for a fleet of thirty-two and the control of all operating costs, budgets and operational efficiency. This included the management of an on-going programme

As captain, on leave with my family before taking my shore post.

of ship-building to replace obsolete vessels with new ones. My decisions affected a work-force, afloat and ashore, of 1,400 men and women.

My education in commercial and business administration began in earnest with a series of residential schools at executive management colleges, and continued with a period of secondment to corporate head offices at New York and Boston to learn the rudiments of American commercial procedures. There were further secondments to shipbuilding and repair yards before I became general manager and director of marine operations, a post which I held for eight years. During this period I was chairman of both the Southampton and Bristol Ship-owners' Association and of the employers' associations of both these ports.

I continued in post until 1976, by which time I had completed thirty years' service and felt that it was time for a change. I accepted an attractive and challenging overseas appointment as general manager, Bahrain. All foreign companies operating in this Gulf state are required by law to secure a national sponsor and my office was sponsored by a member of the Royal House, His Excellency the Minister of Information. As a result, my wife and I enjoyed the privilege of attending most embassy functions, where we met

As marine superintendent, escorting Princess Alice.

ambassadors from various countries and made lifelong friendships. Edwina, was able to enjoy playing bridge with partners from Japan, Korea, Iran, Australia, Egypt and the Lebanon – about as international a circle as it is possible to imagine. They used to play once or twice a week, always during the cool of early morning, beginning their first rubber at 7 a.m.

I remained at Bahrain throughout the construction of what was the largest dry-dock in the world at that time. It had been built specifically to accommodate the world's largest fleet of modern tankers, jointly owned and operated by a consortium of five Arab nations. After four years we returned to London on my appointment as director of operations (Western Hemisphere). After completing fifty years in shipping, I retired in 1990 as corporate director, New Shipbuilding Worldwide. It had been an exciting, interesting and varied career and I was well satisfied to move house and return to Wales. We decided to return to my wife's family home near the sea on the beautiful Gower Peninsula and I turned my attention to relaxing hobbies and frequent visits to family and grandchildren in the United States of America. Well, almost satisfied!

CHAPTER SEVEN

Not quite satisfied. There was an important item of unfinished business. A man may, under the pressure of study, command and commercial activity, put out of his mind the experience of being torpedoed and set adrift in an open boat, but he does not forget it. What had happpened to the friendly enemy who, having sunk my ship, had done as much as he could, within the exigencies of war, to ensure that her crew reached safety? As I sat under my magnolia tree and reflected on my good fortune in being spared to enjoy so successful a life, I wondered whether it might be possible to find out about that man's life and his war. Perhaps he too had survived, returned home and was now reflecting on a very different life-experience.

In 1995, after a good deal of thought, and discussions with family and friends who had urged me to write my story, I began the process of research which eventually revealed the whole story of which a part has been touched upon in earlier chapters. My first step was to contact the main military archive centres of the U.K.: the Ministry of Defence (naval historical branch), the Imperial War Museum, the Royal Air Force, the Public Records Office and the Ministry of Transport (Merchant Navy). I was to discover that keepers of archives are courteous people, with a profound interest in their work and a strong desire to assist the researcher.

However, although I received polite replies from all of these centres, with one exception they regretted that severe manpower cuts made it impossible for them to undertake research on my behalf. They advised me to employ an officially approved researcher. The exception was the Imperial War Museum, where Allison Duffield of their Department of Printed Books confirmed that my ship had been sunk by U156 (Captain Hartenstein) on 19 September 1942 in the South Atlantic Ocean and gave details of the loss of our rescuer, H.M.S. *Spaniard*, by fire and explosion, six months after picking us up. In due course Ms Duffield was able to supply me with details of my ship's armament.

Now that I knew which U-boat had sunk the *Quebec City*, my next move was obvious – to contact the U-boat archive at Cuxhaven. The director of this organisation is Horst Bredow, a Berlin teacher who became an officer aboard a U-boat and was decorated for bravery in action. He was still in hospital after being wounded while manning an ack-ack gun when his vessel set out on a patrol in which it was lost with all hands, leaving him with that sense of guilt which inevitably affects the fortunate survivor. After the war he returned to Berlin, resumed his former profession and, in his spare time, as a matter of duty to his lost comrades, set about discovering what exactly had happened to their vessel and informing their next of kin.

There already existed, at Möltenort, near Kiel, an impressive and poignant memorial to German submariners, comparable to our own Merchant Navy memorial at Tower Hill with its bronze plaques listing every ship sunk between 1939 and 1945, together with the name of every officer and seaman lost. Möltenort's plaques list officers and crew of every U-boat and give brief details of the vessels (the overwhelming majority) that were destroyed. He was determined, however, to establish a comprehensive archive. This, with the assistance of Admiral Dönitz and his family, of the few sailors who had survived and the families of those who had died, he was able to accomplish, initially in his spare time. In due course the job became a full-time one, first at Westerland on the island of Sylt, then at Cuxhaven. It now holds virtually complete records of every one of the 1,171 U-boats which took part in the Second World War.

Horst Bredow was equally courteous, though he was understandably somewhat wary at first. On 10 August 1995, I wrote to him, giving an account of the torpedoing of the *Quebec City*, praising Hartenstein's conduct and asking for further information. He replied on 22 August, thanking me for 'your good words about the behaviour of the commander', giving the position at which *Quebec City* was sunk, revealing that Hartenstein later 'lost his life when his boat U-156 was sunk by an American aircraft' and indicating that the archive contained a great deal more information about 'one of our best U-boat commanders'. On 9 September he sent me information about Hartenstein's military career, a photograph of him receiving the Ritterkreuz from Dönitz on the foredeck of U-156, the account in the log of U-156 of the sinking of the *Quebec City*, and eleven photographs of the U-boat.

I had asked about U.S.Navy records of the sinking of U-156, but Horst Bredow was initially sensitive, even aggressive on the subject: none were available, he said; I must contact U.S. National Archives. I did so, mentioning that I assumed U-156 to have been sunk by 'a Catalina'. I received an extraordinary reply which caused consternation in Cuxhaven. They stated that there was no record of any vessel of that name having ever existed among U.S. forces. 'I hope you did not write them that you got the information from me', wrote Horst Bredow, 'U-156 was not sunk by a ship named Catalina, – it was sunk by an aircraft-type Catalina – and this aircraft belonged to the U.S. Navy VP (Squadron) 53.' Of course, I had written nothing of the kind, having frequently observed Catalinas (seaplanes rather like a Sunderland Flying Boat in miniature) on their North Atlantic patrols.

It was three months before I received a further letter from him (he and his wife had been on holiday). During this time I had been in touch with the Department of the Navy in Washington, and received from them detailed and accurate information (forty-five documents about the sinking of U156) about U-boat activities. Horst was delighted to have the opportunity to get a copy of this, and sent me details of Hartenstein's military history. Of his personal life and family, however, he could tell me nothing:

> As you can read, – he was born in Plauen, – that was long time in the soviet zone, – so I do not know if anybody of his family is still alive, – sorry. I also do not know if he was married or not!

On 21 April he sent me a copy of the *Sunday Express* article (4 August 1963), 'I Ordered Bombing of Survivors' and on 2 May 1996 sent me photographs of the rescuing of survivors from the *Laconia*.

The '*Laconia* Incident' (12 September 1942), during which survivors of the torpedoed troopship were bombed by U.S. aircraft, was a *cause célèbre* of the Second World War, almost comparable with the *Lusitania* incident of World War One. It caused mutual accusations of atrocity between the Allies and the Germans and was to feature as a serious war-crime allegation against the German Grand Admiral Dönitz in the Nürenburg trials held after the war. I found a detailed account in *Geschichte des Weltkrieges 1939-45* (1970) by Léonce Peillard. When I sent a copy to Horst he replied, 'This publication is known to me, – but, please, do not think now "Horst Bredow has everything, – it is not necessary to send him any more . . .".' The Navy Department could not provide information about this or the sinking of U-156, and referred me to the U.S. Airforce operational archives, to whom I wrote on 7 November 1996. They readily provided full details of the latter, but were extremely reluctant to provide any of the former. When I told Horst about this, he wrote: 'I can imagine, that they do not want to give any information about a war-crime against U-156!' Not until March 1997 did the Airforce supply full details (*fifty feet* of micro-film) of the U.S. occupation of Ascension Island and the bombing of U-156 as it was rescuing survivors.

In July 1996 I registered as a member at the Public Records Office and spent five days investigating micro-film relating to naval and Airforce activities at Freetown in September/October 1942. From this I discovered the details of our rescue from Liberia. I also obtained information relating to Dönitz.

By now the former merchant cadet and the former enemy submariner had become good friends. Horst's initial wariness, compounded of a patriotic archivist's understandable resentment at the 'theft' of German naval records (of which he had no copies until I supplied them) and an even deeper seafarer's resentment over the *Laconia* sinking ('But I cannot understand, that always the Germans are the "bad men"') was no more. He at last sent me copies of perhaps the most important (to me as a survivor) documents of all: a photograph, taken through the periscope of U-156, of the view which I could not see from the shower, the actual moment when the torpedo exploded against the *Quebec City* and photographs, taken from the conning-tower, of our lifeboats alongside the U-boat. The position was well summed up in his letter of 27 February 1997:

> I am always glad again, that we as former opponents are comrades and friends now, that we work together to find out the truth, that we do so without bad feelings, – because sailors fighting at the sea have never been 'enemies', but opponents, – and we on both sides did nothing other than our duty!

Time is, indeed, for most of us a great healer, though there are always exceptions, particular in a conflict involving as many atrocities as the Second World War.

Propaganda against the enemy is inevitable in time of war, and false accusations both common and, perhaps, politically necessary for civilian morale. When the U-156 surfaced after torpedoing us, our fears were naturally coloured by what we had heard. But this was in no way confirmed by actual experience of contact with enemy sailors. Contrary to the popular view, there is only one record of a U-boat firing on survivors. Its captain was captured and sternly dealt with: a naval court martial found him guilty and he was executed.

The conduct of Captain Hartenstein, as we had observed it ourselves, had been very different. He was forever ready to assist survivors. My initial favourable impression of him was fully confirmed by the detailed information which I had now assembled from British, German and U.S. official records and I have no doubt that the reader will share it after reading the full account which follows.

CHAPTER EIGHT

Plauen is a city in the south-west corner of Saxony, a region known as the Vogtland (after its thirteenth-century rulers, the Vögte von Weida). That is where, on 27 February 1908, Gustav Julius Werner Hartenstein was born, the only son of Selma Emma and Wilhelm Karl Adolf. He had two sisters, Charlotte and Thea Irena. Plauen had a population of only 5,700 at the beginning of the nineteenth century, but the Industrial Revolution brought so rapid an expansion that by the time of his birth it was a city of 128,000. It became a textile centre, with a world-wide reputation for its lace, *Plauener Spitze*. His was a commercial family, involved in the export business. Although Plauen is 350 miles or so from the sea, and there was no nautical tradition on either side of his family, there had been a naval club in the city since 1899, a consequence of the Naval Bill introduced by von Tirpitz in March 1898 and the expansion of the German navy which followed it. (Erskine Childers' classic thriller, *The Riddle of the Sands* [1903], with its account of a German plan to invade Britain, vividly portrays the British reaction to Germany's developing sea-power).

Werner Hartenstein's ambition to become a naval officer arose during his early childhood. He worked hard at school, where he was particularly successful in the Humanities. In 1926 he applied for a naval officer cadetship, but his application was rejected and he went instead to university and studied law with some distinction. He had not given up his ambition, however, re-applied at the age of twenty and was accepted. He served on the light cruiser *Karlsruhe* and on several torpedo boats. Between 3 September 1939 and 22 March 1941 he completed 65 patrols in the torpedo-boat, *Jaguar*, in the North Sea, the English Channel and the Bay of Biscay. In March 1941 he commissioned U-156 and, in five patrols became one of the most successful commanders, sinking 97,190 tons of shipping. He received six decorations, the highest, the *Ritterkreuz* (Knight's Grand Cross in gold), presented to him on the fore-deck of U-156 by Grand Admiral Dönitz on his return from patrol after the sinking of the *Laconia* and *Quebec City*.

To encourage civilian morale during the Second World War towns and cities in Britain were encouraged to 'adopt' warships (the vessels often bore the town's name) and a similar custom existed in Germany.

Plauen's hero and the coat of arms he was proud to bear on his conning-tower.

The commissioning of U-156 on 3 September, 1941 was a red-letter day for Plauen as well as for Hartenstein and his crew. The ceremony was attended by the Bürgermeister and three city officials together with the president and two senior officers of the naval club. After the official ceremony and the unveiling of the city's coat of arms on the conning-tower, the guests were given a conducted tour of the vessel, then the largest as well as the newest U-boat in the fleet. Speaking that evening at the dinner at the Astoria Hotel, Hartenstein stressed his love for the city of his birth and the honour of going into battle with its crest on his conning-tower. The submarine was presented with an accordion, fifty (*sic*) mouth-organs, gramophone records of songs of the Vogtland and four framed photographs of the city; each member of the crew received a book on the history of the city and region. The dinner-party was cut short, however, by a heavy air-raid by the R.A.F. which obliged everyone to take to the shelters.

On 20 July, 1942, by which time he had been responsible for sinking many thousands of tons of enemy shipping and received a number of decorations, Hartenstein was presented with the Freedom of the City of Plauen. He, his officers and all of his crew were enthusiastically welcomed at the railway station. There was a half-day holiday and the people lined the streets as the whole complement of U-156, led by their commander, marched to City Hall for the ceremony.

Hartenstein was no Nazi fanatic, but a highly trained professional seaman in the highest traditions of the German navy, the service in which Nazism was least influential. From my experience of his behaviour when the *Quebec City* was sunk, I knew him to be hard but humane (had we been aware, when U-156 surfaced, of the events three days earlier, our apprehensions would have been very much stronger than they were). My researches revealed that, from his second patrol, when he shelled oil installations in the Caribbean, at Aruba (Dutch Antilles), he had been prepared to avoid threatening human life wherever possible, even at the risk of endangering his ship and crew.

The attack on oil-tank installations at Aruba was a daring one. It involved entering the harbour submerged and surfacing in mid-harbour and Dönitz's report on the incident was appreciative:

> Very well conducted. The captain's first operation with a new boat. The courage, determination and careful seamanship of the captain ensured that his vessel made an excellent beginning . . .

Hartenstein's log-book reveals that, as he was on the point of opening fire, he observed local people, including women and children, in the line of shot as they made their way to church. He withheld his fire until they had passed by and reached a safe distance. I recognised in this the kind of compassion of which I had personal experience, and discovered subsequently that his anxiety to assist survivors (by no means unique among U-boat captains in the early stages of the war) had led to reminders from Dönitz that he must always put the safety of his ship first and even to severe reprimands for failing, in the Admiral's view, to do so.

The 'Laconia Affair' occurred on his fourth patrol, by which time he had destroyed twenty vessels (about 85,000 tons). Laconia was a Cunarder of 20,000 tons, converted into an armed merchantman and in use as a troopship. There were 2,654 people on board: 436 crew, 268 service personnel (including 80 women and children), and 1,800 Italian prisoners-of-war guarded by 160 Polish ex-prisoners of war from Russia. As a result of the events which followed her sinking, Admiral Dönitz issued the controversial Laconia-Befehl (Laconia Directive) of 17 September, 1942:

> (1) All attempts to rescue the crews of sunken ships will cease forthwith. This prohibition applies equally to the picking up of men in the water and putting them aboard a lifeboat, to the righting of capsized lifeboats and to the supply of food and water. Such activities are a contradiction of the primary object of war, namely, the destruction of enemy ships and their crews.
> (2) The order relating to the taking on board of captains and chief engineers remains in force.
> (3) Survivors are to be rescued only if they possess information of importance to the U-boat.
> (4) Be uncompromising. Bear in mind that our adversaries show no concern for women and children when they carry out bombing raids against German towns.

Allied propaganda naturally portrayed the Laconia Befehl as 'an order to murder' and the British prosecutor at the Nuremberg Trial alleged that it amounted to an instruction to kill survivors in the water. This was, however, rejected by the International Military Tribunal.

On the patrol in which Laconia had been hit, Hartenstein had been part of a wolf-pack of four large Type IXC U-boats (1,000-1,200 tons), accompanied by the 'milch-cow' tanker U-459, which had set out from Biscay ports between 16 and 19 August. Their mission was to disrupt traffic on the vital route around the Cape, and south of latitude 5°. They were under orders to attack only really valuable targets so as to avoid jeopardizing the element of surprise. On 12 September, at 22.07, two torpedoes were launched. The *Laconia*'s hull was torn open, some of her lifeboats were damaged and a number of the Italian prisoners killed. She sank at 23.23, leaving many people struggling in the water.

When U-156 surfaced, cries for help were heard in Italian, and the elation of Hartenstein and his crew at having destroyed a major target must have been deflated by the knowledge that they had put at risk the lives of a large number of Axis soldiers. He set about rescue operations and sent Dönitz a radio message announcing that he had sunk a British liner, but that unfortunately it had had 1,500 Italian prisoners on board. In his *Memoirs*, Dönitz says that 'on receipt of this signal I decided to contravene one of the principles of maritime warfare accepted by all nations. This lays down that the exigencies of action take precedence over all rescue operations. Rescue work is undertaken only provided that it does not interfere with a warship's task . . . and initiated an operation which resulted in the rescue of some 800 of the 811 British and 450 of the 1,800 Italians.' All U-boats within reach were ordered to rescue survivors, the Italians were asked to send one of their submarines to assist and the Vichy government was asked to send surface ships from Dakar.

During the night, U-156 rescued 193 survivors, British and Italian, and the following morning a further 200, who were distributed between those lifeboats which had room for them. At 06.00 Hartenstein sent the following message, *en clair* and in English: 'If any ship will assist the shipwrecked *Laconia*'s crew, I will not attack her, provided I am not being attacked by ship or air force. I have picked up 193 men, 4° 52' South, 11° 26' West. German submarine.' By 15 September four other U-boats and the Italian submarine had joined U-156 and all six submarines had survivors aboard. On 16 September at 11.25 a series of events took place which Hartenstein recorded as follows in the U-156's War Diary:

> 11.25: shortly before arrival of other two boats, four-engined aircraft with American markings, bearing 70°. As proof of my peaceful

Survivors of *Laconia* in a lifeboat.

intentions displayed large Red Cross flag four yards square on bridge facing line of aircraft's flight. Aircraft flew over once and then cruised in vicinity for some time. Made morse signals: 'Where are you?' and 'Are there any ships in sight?' No response. Aircraft flew off in south-westerly direction then returned for a few minutes half an hour later.

12.32: aircraft of similar type approached. Flew over at a height of 250 feet slightly ahead of boat, and dropped two bombs at an interval of about three seconds. While the tow with four lifeboats was being cast off, the aircraft dropped a bomb in the middle of these latter. One boat capsized. Aircraft cruised round in the vicinity for some little while and then dropped a fourth bomb some two or three thousand yards away. Realized that his bomb-racks were now empty. Another aircraft. Two bombs, one of which with a few seconds' delayed action exploded directly beneath control room. Conning tower disappeared in a mushroom of black water. Control room and bow compartment reported making water. Ordered all hands to don life-jackets. Ordered all British to leave the boat. Next – all Italians away, as the battery begins to give off gas. (In any case I had no escape apparatus to give them).

113

13.11: sent out war emergency message on four wavelengths . . .
Returned to the lifeboats, to which I transferred all remaining
survivors. (Some of them required a little gentle persuasion . . .'

I was able to obtain, from the U.S. Air Force Historical Research
Agency, microfilmed material confirming the above. A 'Summary of
Anti-Submarine Attacks in Ascension Area' includes the following
report from a B-24 type aircraft from the highly secret U.S. base on
Ascension Island: 'September 16, 1942 . . . sighted submarine in
position 005° South 011° 40' West. Sub was towing two life boats and
approaching two other life boats. Plane circled submarine and the sub
picked up other life boats and continued on course. A white flag with
a red cross was displayed on conning tower of U-boat . . . At a
position about forty miles south of submarine, plane received
confirmation that no friendly subs had been reported in that area and
orders to sink sub . . . plane made one pass dropping three depth
charges . . . two bombs were dropped, one on either side of sub . . .'

When Hartenstein reported to base at 23.04, Dönitz ordered him
not to risk the safety of his boat, to abandon rescue operations if
necessary and not to rely on the enemy showing the slightest

Laconia survivors alongside U-156.

114

U-156 with 120 survivors of *Laconia* on deck.

Captain Hartenstein addressing his senior officers in conning tower of U-156.

consideration. There was heated discussion at U-boat headquarters about abandoning the rescue-attempts: according to his *Memoirs*, Dönitz 'put an end to the discussion with the words: "I cannot put those people into the water. I shall carry on".' The rescue was completed by Vichy warships and Dönitz makes the further point that no British vessel of any sort came to the rescue of the survivors (this is true, and I have failed to discover why. Freetown was fully aware, from Hartenstein's *en clair* message, if from no other source, of what had happened. There was no question here of protecting 'Ultra' intelligence. Presumably instructions had been received from the Admiralty.) This is the context of the *Laconia Befehl*.

In Nicholas Monsarrat's novel about anti-submarine warfare, *The Cruel Sea*, there is an account of how the corvette captain Ericson, convinced that a U-boat is directly beneath them, drops a pattern of depth charges among swimming British survivors. The *Laconia* Affair showed that, in total war, fact is no less savage than fiction. In 1963 the *Sunday Express*, running a series entitled 'U-Boats to the Rescue', interviewed the U.S. Air Force general, Robert C. Richardson, who had ordered the B-24 to attack U-156: ' "I gave the order to bomb the Laconia survivors," he said. "We did not know there were British among them. But even if we had, it would have made no difference. I would have given the order anyway . . . It was the only decision to make. A simple one – and the right one . . .' Suddenly the general laughed abruptly: "The worst thing of all was we were very disappointed that after all the submarine was not sunk (Ericson's wasn't either) . . . That was real bad." '

Dönitz's official assessment of Hartenstein's conduct concludes that 'This incident gives further proof that, when dealing with such an opponent, humanitarian feelings work to one's disadvantage. One must always give absolute priority to the safety of one's own vessel.'

U-156 left the scene to carry out repairs. She had suffered damage to her periscopes, batteries, direction-finding set, sounding gear and hydrophones, but this was adequately repaired by 16.00 on 16 September. On 17 September Vichy warships which had been released from blockade by the British in Dakar harbour took on board *Laconia* survivors from lifeboats and from other U-boats and an Italian submarine. On 21 September the *Gloire* landed 1,041 survivors at Casablanca. Thus ended an incident in some respects unique in the annals of warfare, illustrative of both the best and the worst features of war: on the one hand the comradeship, once battle is over, of seamen on opposite sides; on the other the dreadful sufferings of the innocent from the torpedoing and subsequent bombing of rescue operations.

On 19 September, U-156 sank my ship. During my researches I was able to obtain a translation of Hartenstein's log report:

18 September, 1942: Crew – still the mood is one of depression. Crew occupied in repairing internal damage from bomb blast.
19 September, 1942: The vessel is now 900 miles southwest of Freetown. At about 04.30, periscope revealed a shadow. Had to be an enemy ship. Called officer of watch and boat to action stations. Must hurry because of approaching dawn-light. Continue to plot enemy's true course. Decision made to stand off at periscope depth and continue plotting sequences (*Quebec City* was zig-zagging) of enemy courses.

At 15.13, stopwatch in hand, Hartenstein ordered the firing of tube 6. Thirty-five seconds later he called out excitedly on the intercom that she had been struck amidships and described how she was listing heavily to starboard and settling in the water. Later he reported anxiously that he was still waiting for her to break up. When the *Quebec City* failed to sink as expected, he remarked, 'A tough ship, not sinking. We shall have to have resort to our guns.' He advised the crew that the enemy ship was heavily armed, then prepared to surface.

As they surfaced, Hartenstein was first into the conning-tower, followed closely by his bridge watch and the armed lookouts we had noticed. He gave the order to steer for the lifeboats, saying, 'I wish to question them and obtain full details.' I have already given an account of what then occurred, and of how he ordered us to move well clear of our ship because he intended to sink her with shell-fire.

His log account of the sinking is as follows: 'Shell after shell went into this death-defying ship. Shots penetrated the waterline and decks, fire broke out and extended throughout, but the defiant ship would not sink.' Fifty-eight shells had been fired before Hartenstein ordered Warrant Officer Max Fischer, the gunnery officer, to use the large calibre forward gun. 'After brief orders, the first shell leaves the barrel with a loud screaming noise, strikes amidships directly above the waterline. Dark smoke billows out from the ship. After seven further shots from the 10.5 gun, coupled with a direct hit on the ship's stern ammunition magazine, there is an explosion and she slowly sinks. We move away at full speed to operate against the La Plata – Freetown traffic.'

I now understood the extremely cautious approach of U-156 and why Hartenstein had not offered us either food or water, why he had made no attempt to assist us in our struggles with the waterlogged lifeboat and what he had meant by being unable to tow our lifeboats.

He could not disobey Dönitz's directive. Neither his, nor his crew's humanity had been affected, however. We were given a friendly greeting, seafarer to seafarer, we were given help and advice about our navigation and the U-156 was certainly put at risk of further air attack by remaining so long on the surface.

The *Quebec City* was Hartenstein's last success. U-156 returned to Lorient on 16 November 1942 and Hartenstein received his Ritterkreuz. Fully repaired, the submarine set out on her final patrol on 16 January 1943. Her destination was the western North Atlantic, off the coast of Brazil to the north-east of Trinidad, Barbados and the Windward Islands. Here she would be well placed to attack vessels entering or leaving the Caribbean or the Panama Canal. In his *Memoirs*, Dönitz stresses that he had repeatedly warned his captains about the danger of air-attack, but they were always inclined to believe that as long as there was no aircraft in sight they were safe and thus fail to allow themselves the necessary time to submerge to a safe depth. In order to be safe, a U-boat had to spot an aircraft while it was still four miles away and to be in a state of readiness, travelling at high speed and with only the watch-keepers on deck. It was, in fact, the increasing effectiveness of air patrols that finally defeated the U-boats.

U-156 returning to Lorient, November 1942.

Grand Admiral Dönitz presents the Ritterkreuz to Captain Hartenstein
on fore deck of U-156 in Lorient.

Hartenstein's last message was transmitted in the early hours of 6 March, 1943 and reported that he had been subjected to intense and prolonged air attack. The enemy, he said, appeared to have developed a new homing device which the U-boat's Metox system could not detect.

U-156 was obliged to remain on the surface to have any prospect of detecting an enemy ship or aircraft in heavy, adverse weather conditions, but to maintain a high enough speed for rapid submersion was impossible. One violent depression after another was sweeping across the North Atlantic, with merciless gales turning it into a desolate waste of mountainous seas. Conditions for the officers on watch were almost unimaginable: waves broke over the conning-tower, they were blinded, soaked and icy cold and it was impossible to keep their binoculars clear.

Two days later, at 13.10 hours, a Catalina flying boat sighted U-156 from a distance of eight miles. She was travelling on the surface, at a speed of 8-10 knots. Cloud cover enabled the aircraft to close to within a quarter of a mile before beginning its attack. Captain Cleary, in the bow turret, opened fire at three hundred yards on a man in a reclining position on the platform aft of the conning-tower. He never got up from this position, though Cleary believed that he had started to do so when he was hit. A man on the deck just forward of the gun started to run towards the bow, threw up his hands and pitched onto the deck. The final burst from the gun was seen to go directly down the conning-tower.

A salvo of four depth charges was dropped from a height of no more than a hundred feet. With the benefit of surprise, and attacking from that altitude, it was virtually impossible to miss. When the charges exploded, the U-boat lifted and broke into two almost equal parts, the centre section going under first, then the bow and stern rising into the air before going under. A violent explosion (presumably of her torpedoes) occurred, sending debris, smoke and water forty feet into the air, leaving behind a patch of foam 150 to 200 feet across which remained for about five minutes. A silvery-green oil-slick appeared around the edges of the foam. After the foam subsided several splodges of heavy brown oil were seen in the centre of the slick, which expanded into a rectangle three-quarters of a mile long and a quarter of a mile wide.

At least eleven survivors were (incredibly) sighted swimming or clinging to wreckage within the slick. Two were on an upright black cylinder or buoy, three in the water and four clinging desperately to another cylinder five hundred feet away. A hundred yards to the north, two men clung to a torpedo-like silver cylinder. These two lost their hold and disappeared almost at once. The four men on the black cylinder also disappeared, leaving five final survivors. Three of them managed to join the two on the upright buoy or cylinder.

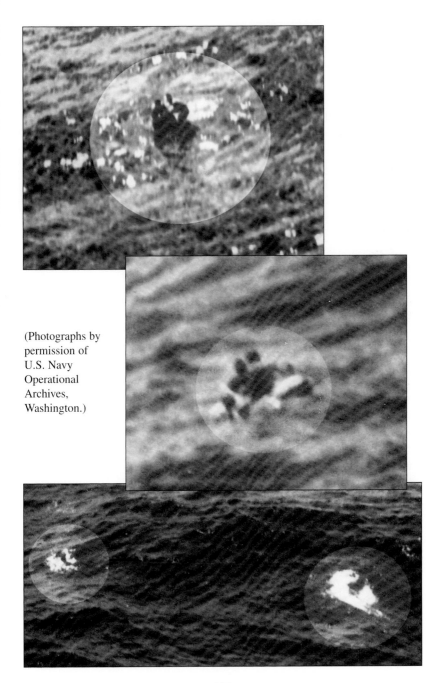

(Photographs by permission of U.S. Navy Operational Archives, Washington.)

121

The airmen's first action was to take six pictures of the scene. A life-raft was then dropped and eventually all five men managed to reach it. Three were sitting on it and the other two hanging on to the sides. A second raft was dropped, but failed to inflate. Before leaving the area an emergency ration kit tied to two inflated Mae West life-jackets was dropped and the survivors were seen to row towards it and believed to have reached it. Four of the survivors were clad only in shorts or bathing trunks; the fifth, possibly an officer, wore a shirt as well. He was heavier and seemed older than the others, who all appeared to be in their late teens. The men waved frantically, trying to persuade the aircraft to land, but the sea was too rough and fuel was low. One man was seen to shake his fist. Seventeen photographs were taken altogether during the hour and thirty-nine minutes the flying boat remained at the scene.

A Spanish freighter, the *Aldecoa España*, had been observed in the general area, but the odds against five men on a small raft being sighted, even in good conditions, were enormous and they all perished, probably within a very short time and almost certainly from exposure.

Latitude 12° 38' North, Longitude 54° 49' West. The North Atlantic, north-east of Trinidad. The enemies we killed, my friends, Korvettenkapitän Werner Hartenstein, Knight's Cross, and his shipmates, lie 3,500 metres deep. 'War is war. It is the duty of each of us to serve his flag and his country.'

On 15 January, 1944, ten months after his death, a service of remembrance for Werner Hartenstein was held at Plauen. It was attended by his parents, Wilhelm Karl Adolf and Selma Emma, by his sisters and other members of the family and by the Bürgermeister, senior officials and councillors. The press report records that 'His parents have accepted that their loving son will not return home but is resting in peace with his Lord.' There, but for the grace of God . . .

POSTSCRIPT

After three years' archive research in Germany, the U.S.A. and London I had obtained sufficient material – military records, documents and photographs – to write my account. This I did while on vacation with my daughter in New England during the autumn of 1997. I returned home with a typescript and computer disk to present to my editor, Don Dale-Jones, who, aptly, it seems to me, described his function as that of a midwife delivering, in a form suitable for the printer, the work so long gestated by its author.

Reflecting on Hartenstein's story during the festive season of 1997-8, I felt that I had done rather well with the military aspects, but less so with the human ones. I knew every detail of his naval career, but nothing of the man except what could be inferred from the brief contact after the torpedoing of the *Quebec City* and from his conduct in actions such as the *Laconia* Affair. I knew his place and date of birth – would it be worth writing to Plauen? But I also knew that Plauen, part of the D.D.R., had been, for 44 years, under the effective domination of the Soviet Union. Not to mention the damage and confusion of Allied bombing and the invasion and occupation of Germany.

Nothing ventured, nothing gained: on 23 January 1998 I addressed a letter to 'Der Oberbürgermeister, City of Plauen, Germany'. In it I referred to my wartime encounter with the U-boat captain born in the city and asked whether they could help with my research. Four weeks later, having received no reply, I concluded that my researching days were over. Then, on 7 March, there arrived a large white envelope bearing the arms that I had seen so long ago on the conning-tower of U-156, those of 'Plauen, Stadt im Vogtland'.

It came from Frau Rober, Archivist, who told me that the Bürgermeister's office had passed my letter to her, and that she had immediately sent a copy to the press officer of the Plauen Naval Comradeship. Here was another surprise: I had thought it unusual that a landlocked city 350 miles distant from the nearest coastline (the Baltic) should produce a naval hero. Apparently it had a naval tradition strong enough to support an association which had been in existence since 1899.

The press officer, Herr Wolfgang Strobel, also wrote to me. He was excited to be in touch with someone who had met the local hero and informed me that the association had only recently been revived. It had been banned from 1945 until 1990.

The cordial exchange of correspondence which followed with both Herr Strobel and Frau Rober revealed that I was not the only researcher with an interest in Hartenstein. A British film producer, Nigel Turner, had recently visited Plauen, they informed me, to gather information for a film about the *Laconia* Incident.

My wife Edwina and I have been invited to Plauen for the three-day Centenary celebrations of the Naval Fellowship in April and May 1999, when the chief of naval staff is to unveil a plaque in Hartenstein's memory. On Day One, I shall present to the Bürgermeister of Plauen a plate bearing the coat of arms of the City of Swansea and a letter from Swansea's Lord Mayor and receive on his behalf a presentation in return. On Day Two, I shall address the 800 members and guests of the Fellowship at the Festival Hall. On Day Three, I shall lay a wreath bearing the silk ribbon of the Swansea British Legion at Plauen's cenotaph. All of these proceedings will receive extensive coverage on German TV and Radio and in the German national press. Video recordings will be made, and I shall receive copies of them.

I have already, at the Fellowship's invitation, submitted a letter about my experience of Hartenstein, and this has been translated and published in their magazine. The regional newspaper, the *Vogtland Auszeiger*, under the headline 'Former Enemies Become Friends' has published a summary of my story, with particular emphasis on the *Laconia* Affair and the Nuremberg Trial. Dr Wolfgang Hess has asked to meet me during my visit to Plauen to discuss the war at sea. Dr Hess supplied the following anecdote from Herr Hetze, principal of Hartenstein's old school: 'It was the most wonderful experience when our respected Captain Werner Hartenstein (Knight's Cross) entered his old boarding-school at the beginning of December 1942 . . . sat down at a desk in Class 7 and answered questions from the boys (instead of a Latin lesson) and (on a second visit) spoke from the lectern in the hall and held us all under his spell . . . (he) could speak for hours at a time of his daily life on the U-156 and of the great days of the U-boat war in the Atlantic . . . we could visualise being there'.

Finally, Horst Roth, a Plauen schoolboy during the War, sent in an account which casts further light on the character of a remarkable man: 'As a schoolboy at Plauen, and then at the Marine School, I was interested in the sea and sea-travel. This led me, as a 14-year-old, to join the Naval Hitler Youth, where we were made familiar with the theoretical and practical aspects of sea-travel.

'During this time, more or less on my own, I built a seaworthy sailing boat in which I ventured out to sea from Dobeneck to the Pertre-Dyke, admired by my friends who, from time to time, I invited to sail with me. I used to cycle from Plauen to Dobeneck . . . We followed the reports of the successes of Commander Hartenstein with great interest. At the appropriate time I submitted myself as a naval cadet to the Naval Command and was, to my delight, accepted.

'In the autumn of 1941, our leader, Schulz, surprised us with the news that two cadets would be invited to Swinemunde . . . this trip would be the greatest event for any of us. We could experience what we had seen in the Newsreels and we would be linked with one of our own, from Plauen, one of our heroes . . . Heinz Wimmer renounced his claim so that I could go. I was grateful to him until the day he died and have never forgotten it . . . we set off, first by train to Swinemunde, Wolfgang Thiel and I, in our Naval Hitler Youth uniforms. We easily found U-156 and were greeted by the crew like old friends. Commander Hartenstein greeted us like a father . . . We were shown around the ship by the commander himself, and nothing was kept hidden. What remains in my memory? The diesel engines, the huge batteries, the torpedo tubes, the stores, the crew's quarters – and everywhere tube-ventilators, control panels. The conning-tower, of course, with its famous ladder. Everywhere there were obstructions to bang your head on. Above all, the strong smell of diesel. The evening meal remains unforgettable. There were Brussels sprouts, the first in my life: now I knew what these splendid little vegetables tasted like – diesel!

'We travelled by night, for security reasons, from Swinemunde across the bay to Kiel. During the trip we were allowed on deck. The engines hammered away with their powerful steady beat that was calming and gave a sense of safety. Above, in the conning-tower, were the lookouts and officers of the watch. The boat rode calm and deep in the water, on a bed of white foam. From time to time we heard the name of a lighthouse or lightship.

'The trip lasted about 160 sea-miles and for a young man who previously had sailed at no more than 2 knots as far as Pertre-Dyke, that was quite something. The whole adventure had so overwhelming an effect on me that I have been obsessed with the sea ever since. I realised that there was a war on, but over all there was a deep peace – diffused, I believe, by Commander Hartenstein. I am deeply grateful to him for his courageous, unorthodox act in taking two schoolboys on this trip.

Quietly, and full of gratitude, we started home by train. Which of us could then have believed that this man, so committed to his duty, would never come home from sea?'

My ship was the last to be sunk by U-156 and it seems that I am now the last living survivor from either side to have stood on the foredeck of U-156 before it was sunk with the loss of my friendly enemy and all his gallant crew. Hartenstein's wish of some 57 years ago, expressed in the lonely expanse of the South Atlantic at that time of bitter conflict, has come true in the right royal welcome I have received from our former enemies. We shall meet at last in peaceful surroundings at his birthplace, the city whose arms I first saw on the conning-tower of U-156.

*   *   *

To understand others is to understand oneself. As a young sailor I experienced at first hand the tragedy of total war between great nations. I had the good fortune to survive the bitter fighting, to learn to put terrible experiences behind me and move forward into a new future in a peaceful world. I give thanks that my life was spared and that I have been able to establish friendly and peaceful relations with our former enemy. I hope that my experiences will be a source of hope to future generations.

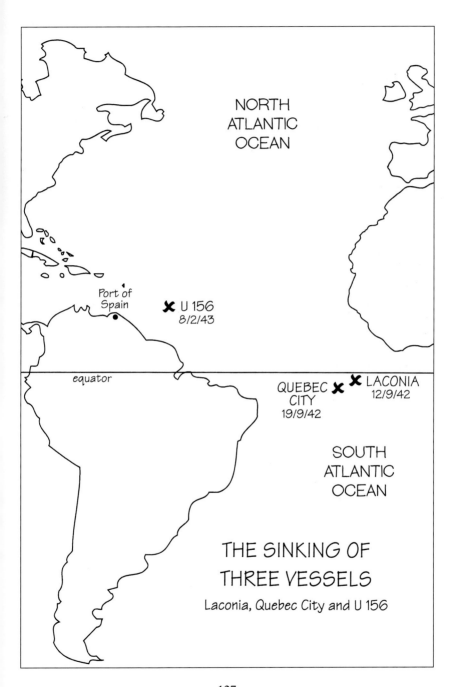

NORTH
ATLANTIC
OCEAN

Port of
Spain

✖ U 156
8/2/43

equator

QUEBEC ✖ ✖ LACONIA
CITY   12/9/42
19/9/42

SOUTH
ATLANTIC
OCEAN

THE SINKING OF
THREE VESSELS
Laconia, Quebec City and U 156

Bibliography

BEKKER, Cajus: *Hitler's Naval War.*
MARTIENSSEN, Anthony: *Hitler and his Admirals.*
DÖNITZ, Grand Admiral: *War at Sea.*
PEILLARD, Leonce: *The Laconia Affair.*
WATTS, Anthony J.: *The U-Boat Hunters.*

Acknowledgements

The author and publishers gratefully acknowledge material from the following sources: Public Records Office, Kew; Ministry of Defence (Whitehall Library); Naval Historical Branch, Scotland Yard; Imperial War Museum, Lambeth; Royal Air Force, Hendon; U-Boat Archive, Cuxhaven, with particular and cordial thanks to my friend, Horst Bredow; U.S. national Archive, College Park, Maryland, who were kind enough to make available fifty feet of microfilmed U-Boat Records captured at the end of the war; U.S. Navy Operational Archives, Washington D.C.

Appendices

I: Summary of Werner Hartenstein's Life

Born	February 27, 1908	Plauen/Vogtland
Died	March 8, 1943	Atlantic, east of Barbados

Sank 19 ships for a total of 97,190 tons.

Decorations

June 6, 1939	Spanienkreuz in Bronze
November 16, 1939	Iron Cross 2nd class (EK II)
April 27, 1940	Iron Cross 1st class (EK I)
February 2, 1942	Deutsches Kreuz in Gold
March 17, 1942	U-Bootskriegsabzeichen
September 17, 1942	Knights Cross (63)

Ranks

January 1, 1930	Fähnrich zur See
April 1, 1932	Oberfähnrich zur See
October 1, 1932	Leutnant zur See (9)
September 1, 1934	Oberleutnant zur See (14)
June 1, 1937	Kapitänleutnant (6)
June 1, 1942	Korvettenkapitän (6)

U-boat Career

U-156	IXC	five patrols, 290 days	09.41–03.43

Werner Hartenstein began his naval career in April 1928. He first served on the light cruiser *Karlsruhe* and then on several torpedo boats, on which he completed 65 patrols in the first years of war. In March 1941 he was transferred to the U-boat force.

On 4 September, 1941 he commissioned U-156. On the second patrol the boat attacked the refinery of Aruba. On the fourth patrol U-156 was involved in the *Laconia* Incident. The boat was sunk by an US Navy aircraft on the fifth patrol, under Harteinstein, with the loss of all hands.

II: The *Laconia* Incident

On September 12, 1942 at 22.07 hours U-156 under the command of Kptlt. Werner Hartenstein torpedoed a large target in the South Atlantic in position 05.05S, 11.38W. The large vessel was the British liner *Laconia* (19,695 tons) which sank at 23.23 hours. The liner was carrying a 136-man crew, some 80 civilians, military material and personnel (268 men) and approx. 1,800 Italian prisoners of war with 160 Polish soldiers on guard.

Radio message from Laconia:
(sent on September 12, 22.22 hours on 600 meters frequency):

> SSS SSS 0434 South/1125 West Laconia torpedoed

Shortly after the sinking the crew of U-156 was amazed to hear Italian voices in the sea amongst the people both in lifeboats and also stuggling in the water itself. Hartenstein immediately began rescue operations and radioed for assistance, both from nearby U-boats and also sent out uncoded messages for every vessel around to assist, promising to cease hostilities.

Radio message from U-156 to BdU:
(sent on September 13, 01.25 hours):

> *Versenkt von Hartenstein Brite 'Laconia' Marinequadrat FF 7721 310 Grad. Leider mit 1500 italienischen Kriegsgefangenen. Bisher 90 gefischt. 157 cbm. 19 Aale, Passat 3, erbitte Befehle.*

Sunk by Hartenstein British 'Laconia'. Grid FF 7721 310 degrees. Unfortunately with 1,500 Italian POW's. Till now 90 retrieved. 157 cubic meters (oil). 19 eels, trade wind 3, ask for orders.

Uncoded message:
(sent on September 13, 06.00 hours on 25 meters-frequency):

> If any ship will assist the ship-wrecked 'Laconia' crew, I will not attack providing I am not being attacked by ship or air forces. I picked up 193 men. 4, 53 South, 11, 26 West.—German submarine.

In the next days U-156 saved some 400 survivors, held 200 on board and the other 200 in lifeboats. On September 15, at 11.30 hours, U-506 under Kptlt Erich Würdermann arrived at the scene and continued to rescue the survivors.

A few hours later U-507 under Korvkpt. Harro Schacht and the Italian submarine *Cappellini* also arrived. The boats headed for shore, towing the lifeboats behind them. Hundreds of survivors were inside the U-boats themselves.

On September 16, at 11.25 hours an American B-24 Liberator bomber operating from the Ascension Island arrived at the scene where its pilot spotted the boats (which at that time flew the Red Cross flag and were clearly not hostile to anyone). The pilot radioed back to his base asking for instructions and was told to attack at once which he did at 12.32 hours, forcing the U-boats to cut the lines to the lifeboats and submerge immediately, leaving hundreds of people again struggling in the water.

Thankfully, this US intervention caused not as much loss of life as it could have as shortly afterwards some neutral French warships from Dakar arrived at the scene and started picking up survivors. Also many had been taken into the U-boats themselves and were safe there, since the bomber failed to sink them. Roughly 1,500 people survived the sinking.

This incident prompted one of the most controversial orders Dönitz ever issued, usually known as the *Laconia* order today. He made it absolutely clear that no U-boats were to take part in any rescue operations from that date and leave any survivors in the sea. Up until that time U-boats had on very many occasions helped the survivors of their victims with supplies, water, directions to nearest land and so on.

Laconia-Befehl (*Laconia* order)

1. *Jegliche Rettungsversuche von Angehörigen versenkter Schiffe, also auch das Auffischen Schwimmender und Anbordgabe auf Rettungsboote, Aufrichten gekenterter Rettungsboote, Abgabe von Nahrungsmitteln und Wasser haben zu unterbleiben. Rettung widerspricht den primitivsten Forderungen der Kriegsführung nach Vernichtung feindlicher Schiffe und deren Besatzungen.*
2. *Die Befehle über das Mitbringen von Kapitänen und Chefingenieuren bleiben bestehen.*
3. *Schiffbrüchige nur dann retten, wenn ihre Aussagen für das Boot von Wichtigkeit sind.*
4. *Bleibt hart. Denkt daran, das der Gegner bei seinen Bombenangriffen auf deutsche Städte keine Rücksicht auf Frauen und Kinder nimmt!*

A translation reads:

> (1) All attempts to rescue the crews of sunken ships will cease forthwith. This prohibition applies equally to the picking up of men in the water and putting them aboard a lifeboat, to the righting of capsized lifeboats and to the supply of food and water. Such activities are a contradiction of the primary object of war, namely, the destruction of enemy ships and their crews.
> (2) The order relating to the taking on board of captains and chief engineers remains in force.
> (3) Survivors are to be rescued only if they possess information of importance to the U-boat.
> (4) Be uncompromising. Bear in mind that our adversaries show no concern for women and children when they carry out bombing raids against German towns.

This order was central to the trial of Dönitz for war crimes at Nüremberg in 1946. Dönitz served eleven years and six months in prison.

III: The History of U-156

Type	IXC	
Laid down	11 October, 1940	AG Weser, Bremen
Commissioned	4 September, 1941	Kptlt. Werner Hartenstein (Knights Cross)
Commander	09.41–03.43	Korvkpt. Werner Hartenstein
Career	5 patrols	09.41–12.41 4th Flotilla (Stettin) 01.42–03.43 2nd Flotilla (Lorient)
Successes	18 ships sunk for a total of 92,889 tons 4 ships damaged for a total of 20,001 tons	
Fate	Sunk at 13.15 hrs on 8 March, 1943 east of Barbados, in position 12.38N, 54.39W, by US bombs (Catalina from USN-VP. 53). 52 dead (all crew lost).	

U-156 sank on September 12, 1942 the allied liner *Laconia* west of Africa in what has become known as the *Laconia incident*.

1st patrol—Krvkpt. Werner Hartenstein
Departure   Kiel, Germany   24 December, 1941 ⎱ *Operational Area*
End of patrol Lorient, France   10 January, 1942 ⎰ North Atlantic
    No Successes

2nd patrol—Krvpt. Werner Hartenstein
Departure   Lorient, France   19 January, 1942   ⎱ *Operational Area*
End of patrol Lorient, France   17 March, 1942   ⎰ Western Atlantic
    and the Caribbean

Successes

Date	Convoy	Nationality	Ship	Tonnage
16 February	EC 69	British	*Pedernales*	4,317 (d.)
16 February	EC 69	British	*Oranjestad*	2,396t
16 February	EC 69	American	*Arkansas*	6,452 (d.)
20 February	ED 64	American	*Deplata*	5,127
25 February	ED 18	British	*La Carriere*	5,685
27 February	DN 95	British	*MacGregor*	2,498
28 February	DO 71	American	*Oregon*	7,017

3rd patrol—Krvkpt. Werner Hartenstein

| Departure | Lorient, France | 22 April, 1942 | *Operational Area* |
| End of patrol | Lorient, France | 7 July, 1942 | Western Atlantic and the Caribbean |

Successes

13 May, 1942	EE 63	Dutch	*Koenjit*	4,551
13 May, 1942	EE 27	British	*City of Melbourne*	6,630
15 May, 1942	EE 66	Japanese	*Kupa*	4,382
17 May, 1942	EE 63	British	*Barrdale*	5,072
18 May, 1942	EE 61	British	*San Eliseo*	8,042 (d)
18 May, 1942	EE 62	American	*Quaker City*	4,961
21 May, 1942	ED 66	Dom. Rep.	*Presidente Trujillo*	1,668
25 May, 1942	ED 66	American	*USS Blakeley (DD)*	1,190 (d)
29 May, 1942	ED 64	British	*Norman Prince*	5,970
3 June, 1942	EE 71	British	*Lilian*	80
24 June, 1942	DQ 11	British	*Willimantic*	4,558

4th patrol—Krvkpt. Werner Hartenstein

| Departure | Lorient, France | 20 August, 1942 | *Operational Area* |
| End of patrol | Lorient, France | 16 November, 1942 | Western Atlantic and the Caribbean |

Successes

27 Aug., 1942	CF 89	British	*Clan MacWirther*	5,941
12 Sept., 1942	FE 77	British	*Laconia*	19,695
19 Sept., 1942	FE 49	British	*Quebec City*	4,745

5th patrol—Krvkpt. Werner Hartenstein

| Departure | Kiel, France | 16 January, 1943 | *Operational Area* |
| End of patrol | Lorient, France | 8 March, 1943 | Mid Atlantic |

No Successes

U-Boot-Archiv

Kiellegung	: 4.10.1940	Typ : IX C
Stapellauf	: 21.05.1941	
Indienststellung	: 4.09.1941	
Bauwerft	: Deschimag Bremen	

Verbleib des Bootes : 8.05.1943 im Mittelatlantik östlich
Barbados durch eine Catalina der
USN VP 53 versenkt.
Boot liegt in 3500 m Tiefe   52 Tote, 2 Einzelverluste

Versenkungsort : 12°38'N 54°39'W   Feldpost Nr. M - 01308

Flottillenzugehörigkeit :
9.41-12.41 4.U-Fl.   12.41-3.43   2.U-Fl.

Kommandanten :

KK Werner Hartenstein 9.41-3.43 +

Wachoffiziere :
OlzS Paul Just   9.41-7.42
OlzS Gert Mannesmann 4.42-11.42
LzS   Dietrich von dem Borne

LzS   Max Fischer   +
LzS   Silvester Peters +
OlzS Leopold Schuhmacher +

Leitende Ing. :
1) Ol(Ing) Wilhelm Polchau   2) KL(Ing) Erich Schulze +

Bordarzt : ___

Obersteuerleute :   Obermaschinisten :
StOStrm Anton Frühling   OMasch Rolf Becker
                              StOMasch Heinz Horl
                              OMasch Herbert Kleinert

2190 Cuxhaven 12 (Altenbruch)
Telefon: (0 47 22) 3 22
Stadtsparkasse Cuxhaven, BLZ 241 500 01
Konto-Nr. 154 203 – nur für steuerlich absetzbare Spenden
Konto-Nr. 154 195 – für alle sonstigen Zahlungen

Stifter und geschäftsführender Vorstand:
Horst Bredow

(By permission of U-boat Archive, Cuxhaven)